Dictionary of
Egyptology

**GEDDES &
GROSSET**

This edition published 1999 by Geddes & Grosset, an imprint of
Children's Leisure Products Limited

© 1997 Children's Leisure Products Limited,
David Dale House, New Lanark Scotland, ML11 9DJ

Text compiled by RLS Limited

Cover photo of Egyptian relief by
R. Strange/PhotoLink courtesy of PhotoDisc

ISBN 1 85534 356 8

Printed and bound in the UK

Introduction

Egyptology, the study of ancient Egypt in all its aspects, is a subject of endless fascination that embraces the beginnings and early stages of human religion, architecture, government, art and organized society. This dictionary is conceived and planned as a non-expert's guide to the subject. The aim has been to keep entries as concise as possible, with cross-references to lead the reader to other topics that help to fill out a particular area of interest.

Egyptology is still very much a subject in which new discoveries are being made. These new discoveries are both pushing back the dates at which 'earliest' information is known and widening the range and adding to the detail of knowledge that we possess about later periods. It is far from being a static field in which everything is known and there are numerous areas in which experts disagree. This book has the straightforward aim of providing as clear an introduction as possible for people who not only want to find out, for example, what the pyramids were for and how they were built, but what sort of people built them and what their everyday life was like.

Egypt is one of the oldest, and by far the best documented, of the ancient civilizations. Evidence of an ordered human society here stretches back far into the Palaeolithic era. Writing was invented in Egypt more than five thousand years ago, and the Egyptians were the first people to develop a systematic calendar. The kingdom of United Egypt arose around 3150 BC and lasted until the very brink of the Christian era, in 34 BC. During this colossal span of time, the nature of the Egyptian state and of Egyptian society changed remarkably little. The Egyptians of the Later Period felt a strong kinship with their remote ancestors who had built the first pyramids. They were a remarkable people, with a deeply entrenched sense of national pride and identity. Literal believers in the divinity of their kings, they nevertheless also had a strong concept of law and justice, within which the kings should exercise their earthly power. They believed, with some reason, that their land was the most favoured one on earth. Its isolation from early neighbours, the stability of its climate and the annual regeneration of its soil by the River Nile all encouraged a settled disposition among the inhabitants, and once they had created for themselves a satisfactory explanation of their place in the universal scheme of things, they were content to lead their lives according to a set of beliefs and rituals that in essence remained unaltered for two and a half millennia.

A profound sense of the continuity of things was felt by the Egyptians. They lived among vast monuments built in the past, and were constantly adding to them and erecting new ones. To them the past lived on; previous generations gathered in an afterworld where each new generation would ultimately join them. The afterworld was not a separate place, and the spirits of the dead surveyed and influenced the living, and in turn had to be nourished and cared for. Their religious system, elaborated in and sustained by a culture based on (normally) secure agricultural prosperity and economic wealth, was the strong but flexible backbone of the nation, enabling it to preserve its resiliency through the unchanging years and many periods of turmoil and invasion. Such were the people whose culture, history and achievements are the subject of this dictionary.

Throughout the entire period from the First Dynasty to the Thirtieth, there is no recorded history of Europe north of the Alps. As the centuries passed, the Stone Age gradually merged into the Bronze

Age (introduced to northern Europe around 2000 BC). The people who first assembled the stone circles at Avebury and Stonehenge are unknown, their language a matter of surmise. They lived a pastoral existence in huts on the windy uplands whilst far away the Egyptians harvested their corn, made their wine, wrote down their thoughts, and made and decorated great and complex buildings. There were civilizations as old, or older, in Sumeria and China, in some ways more inventive and forward-looking than the Egyptians (who learned from Sumer), but they lacked the stability of the Egyptian system. The civilization of the Indus Valley rose, flourished and fell as Egypt proceeded (not without troubles) from Old Kingdom to Middle Kingdom. The Egyptians of the Middle and New Kingdoms watched the rise and fall of the Middle Eastern empires: Hurrian, Hittite, Mitannian, Babylonian, Assyrian and Persian, and survived conquest and occupation by the two last. The Trojan War was a distant flicker on Egypt's horizon in the spacious days of Rameses II, and two hundred years later, Solomon's glory was underlined by his marriage to a princess of Egypt. When a few pastoral communities banded together to make the first settlement at Rome, around 1000 BC, the Egyptian kingdom was more than two thousand years old. Its religion was ancient when the Greek pantheon was established, when Hinduism appeared and when Gautama Buddha was born, around 560 BC. During the centuries of Egypt's slow decline, the Celts migrated across Europe, bringing the Iron Age to Britain during the 4th century. It was as a still-functioning state that Egypt passed into the last and greatest pre-Classical empire, that of Alexander the Great, in 333 BC. Even then it lived on, independent, although devoid of influence and glory, for another 300 years, until that upstart among empires, the Roman, gathered it in and turned it into a vast granary to feed the population of the metropolis.

A

Abu Ghurob

Site in the SAQQARA area, on the west bank of the NILE, south of Cairo, of the SUN TEMPLE of the Pharaoh Neuserre (FIFTH DYNASTY) and the best guide to the appearance of the now vanished sun temple of HELIOPOLIS.

Abu Simbel

Site in NUBIA of two rock-hewn temples which are among the best-known images of Egypt, ever since the campaign to preserve them when the ASWAN High Dam was under construction in the 1960s and the resulting lake threatened to submerge them. Placed on the west bank of the NILE, 760 miles (1,223 kilometres) south of MEMPHIS, they reflect the movement of grand-scale ARCHITECTURE into and beyond UPPER EGYPT as the Dynasties wore on. They were constructed in the reign and at the behest of Pharaoh RAMESES II, and, although dedicated to HATHOR and HORUS, there is no doubt that they also were intended to proclaim the greatness of the god-king Rameses. Four COLOSSAL STATUES of the pharaoh are positioned outside the larger of the temples, rising to a height of 65 feet (20 metres). Behind the statues, a pylon gate 100 feet (30 metres) high is cut from the cliff face, and the temple extends behind it, 180 feet, (55 metres) into solid rock.

Abusir
Funerary site on the left bank of the NILE, close to MEMPHIS. There are a number of PYRAMIDS, including those of NEFERIRKARE and Neuserre (FIFTH DYNASTY).

Abydos
Site in UPPER EGYPT, to the west of the NILE, about 100 miles (160 kilometres) northwest of THEBES, the location of tombs from the earliest dynasties onwards. With stone quarries conveniently close, it became a major temple and funerary centre and was particularly famed, from the FIFTH DYNASTY onwards, as the cult centre of OSIRIS, whose heart was said to be buried there. During the FIRST INTERMEDIATE PERIOD, both Thebes and HERAKLEOPOLIS fought fiercely to gain control of Abydos and so obtain association with the prestige of Osiris. Temples, tombs and chapels were built at Abydos right up to the end of the dynastic period.

adoratrice of Amun
During the Libyan rule (FIFTEENTH DYNASTY), the kings placed their own candidate in the position of high priest of AMUN-RA at THEBES, effectively creating a VICEROY in UPPER EGYPT. The tendency of these appointees to create their own power base was a problem that the kings sought to resolve by appointing a female chief PRIESTESS instead. These functionaries were known as the adoratrices, or divine worshippers, of AMUN-RA, and they held the role until the end of the THIRTIETH DYNASTY.

afterlife
The Egyptians maintained a firm belief in the afterlife. Indeed, the concept was basic to their civilization, with its tremendous emphasis on preparation for the life to come. DEATH was a stag-

ing point in the flow of existence—a difficult one, beset with dangers and unknown hazards. In the royal despotism of the OLD KINGDOM, there were two kinds of afterlife—the ascent to heaven and the gods, open only to the king and a select few, and an ill-defined, gloomy subterranean existence for everyone else. One of the products of the social disorder that accompanied the end of the Old Kingdom was a breakdown of this segregation. While kings retained a special place in heaven, eternity was also open to others who could afford the necessary rites. The concept of the afterlife became a kinder one, envisaged as a continuity of mortal life, with all its pleasures, activities, and privileges. *See also* UNDERWORLD.

Afrit

A desert spirit embodied in the whirlwind summoned up by SETH.

agriculture

For all her GOLD and minerals, the chief wealth of Egypt lay in her 'black land', or *khemet*, the rich tillage fertilized each year by OSIRIS through the NILE flood or INUNDATION. After its end as an independent kingdom, Egypt became the granary of Rome, but throughout the dynasties, she consumed had this annual wealth herself. (There were instances of corn being supplied to Meso-potamian kingdoms when these suffered famine, but the quanti-ties cannot have been large and were more likely to have been gifts to the court than to the mass of people.) During the OLD KINGDOM, it is likely that only one crop a year was raised. The grain crops were barley and the primitive wheat known as emmer, of more than one type as farmers evolved strains from the origi-nal wild crop. They sowed seed in November, with the onset of the mild winter season, scattering it from small wicker baskets suspended from their shoulders and using their flock of sheep or goats to tread it in, although as the plough came into general use it was ploughed in. The basic field tool was the hoe, made of wood, with the handle jointed to the wooden blade and further secured with fibre twine. During March the corn would ripen. Reapers would cut it with flint-bladed sickles unchanged from the PRE-DYNASTIC PERIOD, tie it up in sheaves and load the sheaves on to donkeys. Some tomb decorations record in hieroglyphic script the remarks of farm-workers, in a manner not unlike that of contemporary strip cartoons. The FIFTH-DYNASTY tomb of Sekem-ankh-Ptah notes remarks like 'Jab him in the backside!' as advice given to a donkey-driver, or an overseer's call, 'Hurry up, our wheat is ready'. The cut corn was taken to a stone threshing floor and threshed by driving cattle or donkeys round and round over the sheaves. All these tasks were for men, but women took over for the winnowing process of separating the chaff, either by shaking the grain in wooden sieves or by waving broad wooden winnowing fans to blow away the chaff. Finally, the grain was measured, the quantity recorded, perhaps with an official present if it were a large farm or yield, and it was stored in the granary or shipped off to a larger grain store. At the same time as the grain crop, flax was grown and harvested, and the dusty process of combing the fibres begun (*see* TEXTILES).

Cattle were bred in large numbers and provided the community with meat, milk and hides as well as draught oxen for ploughing and pulling. Cattle were of such economic importance that they formed part of the regular census. They were a source of anxiety in that they were subject to disease, and herds were often decimated by forms of foot and mouth disease, causing farmers to import breeds from outside Egypt to strengthen the stock. There

Aha

were no grassy plains for animals to graze on, although grass was grown wherever possible, especially in the DELTA and on the slopes of the broad banks between the river and the flooded irrigation basins, so cattle had to be provided with fodder. On a large estate this was a major undertaking—herds could run into several hundreds.

Fruit and vegetables were grown in garden plots. These included salad plants, such as lettuce, and onions, garlic, cucumbers, beans, leeks, lentils and melons. Orchards were set aside for fig trees and vines. BEES were kept for their honey, which had many uses as a sweetener.

Aha

The first known king of a unified Egypt, from around 3150 BC. His reign marks the beginning of the dynasties. He is also known as Meni and Narmer. *See also* FIRST AND SECOND DYNASTIES.

Ahmosis

First king of the NEW KINGDOM and EIGHTEENTH DYNASTY, coming to power around 1550 BC. The first campaigns of his reign marked the end of the HYKSOS domination. He was a warrior king, keen to restore Egyptian prestige, which the Hyksos dominion had severely undermined. He took Egyptian armies on expansionist campaigns through Palestine and also regained control of NUBIA, setting the pattern for the imperial style of the New Kingdom.

akh

One of the five elements forming the human being seen as an aspect of the sun, the link between the human and the luminous life force. It left the body at DEATH to join the circumpolar stars. In HIEROGLYPHICS it is denoted by the crested ibis.

Akhenaten *or* Amenophis IV

(Ruled 1352–1338 BC) Son of AMENOPHIS III, after a period of co-regency with his father, he assumed sole reign, with NEFERTITI as his queen, and, from his second year as absolute monarch, set about a drastic revision of the time-honoured royal cult of AMUN-RA. He built a new temple at KARNAK to the ATEN, but in his fourth year as king began to build a completely new capital city and national cult centre, named Akhetaten ('horizon of the sun disc'), on the east bank of the Nile. Its site, AMARNA, is six miles (ten kilometres) south of present-day Mallawi. In size and splendour, he intended it to outdo THEBES or MEMPHIS. At this time he changed his names to affirm his god-identity with that of Aten. Amenophis means 'Amun is satisfied', whilst AKHENATEN means 'glory of the Aten'. All references to Amun were expunged, and the 'hidden' god was replaced by the 'visible' god. Like most revolutionary steps, this was the culmination of a trend, given pace by an all-powerful and determined individual. Its impact on the general population was slight, but the reaction of the conservative upper classes, and especially the priests, can be gauged by the ferocity with which all traces of Akhenaten's activities were wiped out after his death. It is possible to overestimate the extent of the changes he imposed. Even the great temple of the Aten, its open-air altar so unlike the classic Egyptian concept of the temple, with its inner recesses shrouded and mysterious, harked back to the SUN TEMPLES of the FIFTH DYNASTY. The king himself remained the high priest and intermediary between god and people. The administration of the country went on very much as before. Distinctive developments in the arts, although again part of a growing trend rather than a sudden change, reflect the tastes of the court. There was a move towards 'naturalism'. This was reflected in literature by an easing

11

of the conventions that had kept MIDDLE KINGDOM Egyptian as the written language, ignoring the changes in everyday speech. Now the spoken language was allowed to be written in official documents, and the written language evolved rapidly at this time, a process that the anti-reformists who followed Akhenaten could not reverse. In ART, too, there was a greater freedom of line and realism of portrayal, notably in portrayals of the pharaoh himself.

Akhenaten reigned for some 14 years, perhaps with a co-ruler forced on him at the end, when it had become apparent that his reforms could not be sustained. The image of a king preoccupied with his priest role and the arts is reinforced by the diplomatic letters left at the Amarna site, which testify to the erosion of the Asian empire created by his EIGHTEENTH DYNASTY predecessors. His successors returned to the old capital at MEMPHIS. El-Amarna was emptied of people and possessions and became a ghost city. Much of its stone was removed to form new buildings in the city of HERMOPOLIS MAGNA, facing it on the western bank. Official edicts announced the restoration of the cult of Amun-Ra and condemned the mistakes and crimes of Akhenaten. The monolithic power of tradition resumed its sway. *See also* TUTANKHAMUN.

Akhetaten *see* AMARNA.

Alabaster
Aan easily worked white stone, quarried at a number of sites in MIDDLE EGYPT, notably at Alabastronpolis (Greek: 'city of alabaster') and used to make decorative bowls, vases and statues.

Alexander the Great
(356–323 BC) The Macedonian king who brought most of the Near East under his rule in an empire that reached from Greece

to India. With his conquest of the Persians in 333 BC, he acquired Egypt, at that time under the SECOND PERSIAN OCCUPATION. It was as a result of Alexander's conquests that the Ptolemies ruled Egypt. On the death of Alexander, his enormous dominions were divided among his principal lieutenants, and PTOLEMY Lagos received Egypt and founded the last dynasty, whose kings were wholly Greek. *See also* MACEDONIAN DYNASTY.

Alexandria

The capital of Ptolemaic Egypt and the first really large city of Egypt. It was named in honour of ALEXANDER THE GREAT, who founded it.

Amarna (Tel-el-Amarna)

This site in MIDDLE EGYPT, downstream from THEBES, was chosen by the EIGHTEENTH-DYNASTY Pharaoh AKHENATEN as his new capital when, in a move unprecedented in Egypt's long history, he abandoned Thebes, where his ancestors had been kings, to found not only a new capital but a new centre of worship for a new, or at least newly invigorated, god. He commanded the building of the great temple of Aten, dedicated to the sun disc, as a replacement of the cult of AMUN-RA. The temple form was similar to the traditional one, except for one striking aspect: the sanctuary of the god, instead of being dark and mysterious, was open to the sky. The new city was named Akhetaten, and in the relatively brief span of Akhenaten's reign, it comprised a large number of ceremonial buildings and avenues, together with barracks of workers' houses on the periphery. The palaces and temples were constructed of relatively small stone blocks, which speeded up their building and, not long after, their demolition. A substantial number of inscribed clay tablets, the Amarna Letters, were found on the site, providing much information

Amarna Period

about international relations between the Middle Eastern empires around 1300 BC.

Amarna Period

A period of the NEW KINGDOM, 1348–1336 BC, corresponding to the reign of AKHENATEN, which was centred at his capital on the site of el-Amarna. The Amarna Period saw distinctive changes in the arts of sculpture and painting.

Amasis *see* TWENTY-SIXTH DYNASTY.

Amenophis I

EIGHTEENTH-DYNASTY king (ruled 1526–1506 BC), son of AHMOSIS, who benefited from Ahmosis's conquests. His death marked a change in temple ARCHITECTURE; from now on, the king's MORTUARY TEMPLE was not linked to his tomb, which was physically distant from it. Royal mortuary temples were built on the west bank of the NILE in the Theban area, whilst the tombs were placed in the VALLEY OF THE KINGS.

Amenophis II

EIGHTEENTH-DYNASTY king (ruled 1425–1401 BC). The successor to the great TUTHMOSIS III, he is remembered for his great physical strength and for a degree of cruelty unusual in Egyptian monarchs. Faced with a revolt in Egyptian-held Syria on his accession, he had seven Syrian princes slaughtered in front of the statue of AMUN-RA at THEBES, hanging six bodies on the city wall and sending the seventh to NAPATA, the Nubian capital, as a warning against rebellion. He conducted three military campaigns into Syria and is buried in the VALLEY OF THE KINGS. Some time after his death, his rock tomb was made a place of refuge for the mummies of six later monarchs to protect them from tomb robbers.

Amenophis III

King of the EIGHTEENTH DYNASTY (ruled 1390–1352 BC) and a prodigious builder whose monuments span the country from NUBIA to BUBASTIS and include the colossal baboon statues at Hermopolis and the gallery of the sacred APIS bulls at Saqqara. In the Temple of MUT of Asheru, south of KARNAK, he had 600 statues of the lioness-goddess SEKHMET set up. He constructed a vast MORTUARY TEMPLE for himself on the west bank of the NILE at Malkata, which was later dismantled by Pharaoh Merneptah to provide stone for his own temple, leaving only the two COLOSSAL STATUES that once stood before the gate, the so-called COLOSSI OF MEMNON. Inheriting a strong empire from his predecessors, Amenophis did nothing to enlarge it and was content to lead a life of extreme opulence and luxury. One of his pleasures was to sail in his yacht, *Splendour of the Aten*, on an ornamental lake in the grounds of his palace. His reign was largely peaceful and he enjoyed great international prestige, more as a result of Egypt's status as the greatest power in the region than for his personal qualities. His mother was a MITANNI, and he himself acquired two other Mitanni princesses as wives, as well as two Babylonian princesses. Egypt was very much open to eastern influences in religion, ART and other fields at this time. His principal wife, TIY, mother of his successor, AKHENATEN, was an Egyptian commoner whose father was Master of the Stud Farms. She was elevated to a special status as Great Royal Wife.

Amenophis IV *see* AKHENATEN; EIGHTEENTH DYNASTY.

Ammenemes I

MIDDLE KINGDOM pharaoh of the Twelfth Dynasty (ruled 1991–1962 BC) who was assassinated as the result of a conspiracy that

Ammenemes II, III and IV

began in the women's quarters. The details of this are obscure, but it indirectly prompted one of the most popular literary texts, much used in schools, *The Story of* SINUHE.

Ammenemes II, III and IV *see* TWELFTH DYNASTY.

amphora (*plural* amphorae)

A tall pottery vase used to hold and conserve liquids, including wine and every kind of oil. They were given stoppers of hard mud and paste, marked with a seal to indicate content, ownership and age. The broken shards of amphorae, heaped in middens and tips, are among the most common relics of ancient times. These potsherds were often used by trainee scribes to write and draw on, and so can have added archaeological value.

amulet

A personal charm, often in the shape of an animal or animal-god, intended to procure the wearer certain benefits or to ward off evil spirits that might bring disease or bad luck. These could be simple clay objects or beautifully made, bejewelled ornaments.

Amun and Amun-Ra

In the Hermopolitan COSMOLOGY, Amun was the 'hidden god', a member of the OGDOAD of creation. Despite this auspicious start, Amun remained a local Theban deity for many centuries, but THEBES was a royal city, and its god had wide prestige. Amun was taken up by the kings of Thebes as a war-god. This was during the troubled years of the FIRST INTERMEDIATE PERIOD, between the fall of the OLD KINGDOM and the establishment of the MIDDLE KINGDOM. Amun procured victory for them and was thereafter associated with RA as Amun-Ra. This assimilation with Ra, the supreme sun-deity, conferring national status, also served a useful theological purpose in giving the powerful but remote Ra a human-like persona, which could receive offerings and which could impregnate a queen with the divine seed and so ensure that a pharaoh was 'son of Ra'. Amun-Ra's own associate gods were the vulture-goddess, MUT, and their son, KHONSU. Throughout the Middle and the NEW KINGDOMS, his cult grew, and he had vast and lavish centres of worship at Thebes (LUXOR), KARNAK and MEDINET HABU. Kings of the EIGHTEENTH DYNASTY, most notably AKHENATEN, sought to reduce the power of the high priest of Amun-Ra, and the cult of Ra-ATEN, the 'visible sun', was propagated, but with no lasting success. By the end of the New Kingdom, Amun-Ra was the most powerful god in the Egyptian pantheon, his temples were hugely wealthy and his high priest correspondingly influential. During the THIRD INTERMEDIATE PERIOD, UPPER EGYPT became a theocracy ruled by the priesthood of Amun-Ra, who made their decisions according to the ORACLE of the god.

Amyrtaeus *see* TWENTY-EIGHTH DYNASTY.

Andzti *see* OSIRIS.

Anedjib *see* FIRST AND SECOND DYNASTIES; SED FESTIVAL.

Ani
Author of the *Maxims of Ani*, a widely copied text of the NEW KINGDOM period, drawing on earlier models, intended to lead the reader towards the harmonious life so much appreciated by the Egyptians.

animal cults
Animals are inextricably interwoven with Egyptian religion. Most

of their oldest gods had animal features and probably began as
wholly animal in form. This later underwent a degree of humani-
zation, with animal heads set upon human bodies. However, in
addition to this, there were many instances of animal worship,
either local or national. Bulls, rams, CROCODILES, ibex and fal-
cons were all identified with gods, often, as with bulls and rams,
with more than one deity. Such animals have a certain grandeur
of their own, as well as a strong association with virility, wealth
and fertility. Perhaps the jackal and the CAT fell into this category
too. But far obscurer creatures, the BEE, the ichneumon fly and
the dung beetle, were also treated with reverence and regarded
as sacred. In the activities of these creatures, the Egyptians perceived a particular and intriguing aspect of the life force, linking
insects to the gods in a striking and memorable way, like little
living parables (*see* SCARAB). The Egyptians felt that the god might
manifest itself on earth in the form of the locally worshipped
animal, and these were consequently sacred within the NOME, with
severe penalties for anyone who should harm or kill it. Such constraints applied only within the temple's area of influence. It is
likely that the animal element in the Egyptian pantheon also
makes a link with the ancient past of the peoples who came into
the NILE Valley from central Africa, another region where animal cults were and, to some degree, still are maintained. Animal
cults were far from exclusive to Egypt and existed in cultures
with which the Egyptians had no contact, notably India.

animal life
(1) *domesticated* the ancient Egyptians domesticated the wild
ox, sheep and the goat. The ox stemmed from the long-horned
wild ox (*Bos primigenius*) and was a common beast of burden

long before it was ever hitched to a plough. The sheep was descended from the red-fleeced mouflon (*Ovis musimon*). Most common after the ox was the ass, also a beast of burden. Mule trains carried goods from the Red Sea coast or on portage round the Nile cataracts. The horse arrived in Egypt with the advent of the HYKSOS invasion, and the Egyptians adopted it with eagerness, especially for use with chariots, in sport, hunting and warfare. Dogs existed, both wild and tame. Dog breeding was practised, and the Saluki dog can already be seen in tomb paintings.

(2) *wild* in the PRE-DYNASTIC PERIOD and the OLD KINGDOM, when part of the NILE Valley remained untamed jungle, there was a wide variety of animal life, including elephant, hippopotamus, wild ox, giraffe, panther, leopard and okapi, as well as CROCODILE. Most of these animals were extinct in the region by the early centuries of the Old Kingdom, at least in LOWER EGYPT. In the desert areas there were lions, gazelles, ibex and jackals. For all their reverence for the life force and their appreciation of the divine in animals, the Egyptians were exuberant and skilful hunters, as much of their ART attests, hunting for pleasure as well as for the larder.

Anti

A falcon-god, associated with war, worshipped in UPPER EGYPT, with his cult centre at Deir-el-Gebrawi.

Anubis

A god of the dead, portrayed as a man with the head of a jackal. Originally a deity of UPPER EGYPT, his cult was subsumed into that of OSIRIS (whose origins were in the DELTA) during the MIDDLE KINGDOM. He shared with Osiris the title of Prince of the West (i.e. the place where the dead were). *See also* UNDERWORLD.

Anzti

An ancient DELTA god whose cult centre was at BUSIRIS. Uniquely among NOME deities, he was represented in human form, bearing the crook of a shepherd and the whip of a cowherd. He is depicted in the PYRAMID TEXTS but not later. His cult was absorbed into that of OSIRIS, who took over his emblems and his role, eventually on a national scale. The pyramid text depictions of Anzti are of interest for their display of him in 'mutilated' form—head, shoulders and arms only, with one attenuated leg. This was a precautionary measure. A portrayal of his entire body might risk his coming to life and harming the tomb's occupant. Wild animals were similarly rendered harmless.

Apiru

A tribe or tribes of displaced persons who lived in Egypt during the later NEW KINGDOM, identified by some writers as the exiled Hebrews. *See also* EXODUS.

Apis

A bull-headed god, worshipped in MEMPHIS at the SERAPEUM.

Apophis

A god who personified the negative force of darkness against the light of RA, attacking the sun-god's sky-ship during the darkness of night but always repulsed by dawn. Certain HYKSOS kings also bore the name (*see also* FIFTEENTH, SIXTEENTH AND SEVENTEENTH DYNASTIES).

Apries *see* TWENTY-SIXTH DYNASTY.

architecture

The materials available for building in Egypt were the reeds of the

DELTA area, the muds and clays of the NILE valley, and the different bedrocks that lay beneath or rose up from the ground. Perhaps at a very early stage there was timber enough to have a timber architecture, of which almost nothing survives. It is notable that early rock-cut tombs in cliff faces show an attempt to imitate timber structures, with lintels and door jambs, something common in Asia Minor also. In the same way, the monumental curved cornices so typical of Egyptian temples have been traced back to the reed buildings of the Delta and marshes, where bundles of reed, assembled and tied together, produced a similar effect on a far smaller scale. Outside the Delta area, buildings from the PRE-DYNASTIC PERIOD onward were chiefly of mud brick. The durability of stone, which has preserved so many splendid monuments, should not obscure this fact. It was in the period of the kings, when central organization and despotic rule made it possible to command a large labour force, that building in stone on a grand scale began. From its earliest beginnings, Egyptian stone architecture showed a quality of massiveness and bulk. This had some practical reasons. In a land prone to minor earthquake shocks, it was felt that large buildings should be of solid construction. Because of uncertainty on such matters as load-bearing, the distance between columns was at first deliberately small. The conservatism of Egyptian society tended to preserve such features, even after technical skill and knowledge could have achieved something different. The massive nature of the buildings was accentuated by the 'batter' of their design, i.e. they tended to be wider at the base than at the top, a pattern reflected also in doorways. Indeed, the essentially unchanging style of Egyptian architecture is one of its unique aspects. The superb achievements of the THIRD and the FOURTH DYNASTY seem to have attained the ideal expression of religious architecture, and once that was established, change might be dangerous. There were, however, inevitably some developments through the immense duration of the dynasties, caused by changing circumstances and tastes. The painstaking thoroughness of the early dynasties' workmanship, achieved by remorseless supervision, was only rarely equalled in later times.

Egyptian architecture as we know it is overwhelmingly the architecture of DEATH and religion. Aware that their lives on earth were short, the Egyptians spent more thought, resources and effort on the dwellings that were meant to see them through eternity. Our information on domestic dwelling houses prior to the NEW KINGDOM is limited and comes from models and pictures found in tombs, analogies with tombs and from a few ill-preserved remains. Even the PHARAOHS lived in houses less splendid than the tombs that awaited them. It was rare for a house to have more than two storeys. To the end of the ancient Egyptian period, the vast majority of houses had a ground storey only. The architecture associated with the OLD KINGDOM is chiefly that of the PYRAMIDS and of MASTABAS. The mastaba was the first true expression of Egyptian architecture. Originally it was a simple structure that marked and sealed the pit where an important person was buried. It developed into a building in its own right, made of stone by the time of the FOURTH DYNASTY rather than mud brick, with at first one room then eventually several rooms, all of them furnished and decorated. The earliest pyramids were of stepped construction, rising in a series of ledges and, like that of SAQQARA, which is oblong in plan, not always set on a square base. They owe their origin to the mastaba, which in its later form was often a very large construction. The later pyramids are true geometrical pyramids, rising smoothly to a point.

The architect was a court functionary whose job was not to innovate but to replicate, interpret and, under ambitious pharaohs, to do what had been done before, but bigger. The few truly original buildings that have come down the ages to us, like the Step Pyramid, stand out for their originality. Originality was not seen as a good thing by the Egyptians, at least after the period of the pyramids. Architecture was not prized in its own right as an ART, but as a means of expressing the liturgy and of praising the gods. As a result, long after they could have employed more daring designs and more sophisticated tools, the designers of Egyptian buildings followed tradition as slavishly as if they were walking a tightrope. Nevertheless, their work has remained a marvel to succeeding generations, and we still count the Great Pyramid among the Wonders of the World. *See also* HOUSE, TEMPLE, TOMB.

Armant

An important PRE-DYNASTIC PERIOD site, cult centre of the god MONTU, in the heart of Theban territory.

army

The Egyptians did not take readily to being soldiers, and during the OLD KINGDOM there was a very small standing army. Military leadership was considered as just one of the skills of a successful administrator (*see* WENI). The Egyptians brought in recruits from desert tribes as guards and law enforcers, on the basis that foreigners could be better relied on to serve the government. Corruption on a petty scale was endemic in Egypt, and local guards would have been unreliable. Conscription was necessary to gather a substantial army together. The system is seen at work when the TWELFTH-DYNASTY king, AMMENEMES I, appointed the NOMARCH of the Oryx NOME as Great Director of Soldiers, in which capac-

art

ity he had to bring up to 600 selected men to take part in an expedition into NUBIA. In the NEW KINGDOM and LATE PERIOD, when massive armies were common, a distinct military class appeared for the first time. Successful leaders on land and sea were rewarded with slaves and property. There were special decorations for distinguished military service. Pharaoh Rameses II, in his reproach to the soldiers who almost lost him the battle at Kadesh, said, 'There is not one man among you to whom I have not given a good portion on my land . . . I have relieved you of your taxes . . .', the implication being that there were privileges available to the common soldier as well. At this time the Egyptians also used foreign mercenaries on a large scale—Greek, Jewish, Libyan and Nubian. *See also* MILITARY ORGANIZATION.

art

Painting in ancient Egypt was a craft rather than an art, as art is understood in modern times. Its function was to display, inform and decorate, but the decoration invariably had a practical purpose, whether it was to demonstrate the greatness of a PHARAOH or to illustrate some simple process like fish-spearing. In effect, painting was the extension of hieroglyphic writing, on a larger surface, with different materials. The typical form of painting was the fresco, painted directly on to the inner walls of tombs, temples and large houses. The colours were sometimes applied directly to the wet plaster, but more often on to a specially prepared wall dressing of gypsum, or chalk plaster, mixed with gum in order to create a smooth surface. The paints were made from dry cakes of mineral-based pigment, mixed with water and a resinous gum. The colours were bright and strong, reflecting the sharp clarity and vivid colours of the sunlit landscape outside.

Black, blue, brown, green, grey, red, white, yellow and pink were employed in the range, the last being a late NEW KINGDOM introduction. Application was made with a fibrous wood implement the ends of which could be teased into a brush-like formation. When planning the painting of a large surface, the painter, or master painter in charge of a team, divided the space into a series of registers, and within each, the figures and inscriptions were carefully plotted, with small squares marked out in red or black to act as guidelines for scale and content. This grid was unvarying through most of ancient Egyptian history, until the TWENTY-SIXTH DYNASTY (663–525 BC), when the proportions of the figures were altered to a taller, more slender schema. In the standard grid arrangement, every part of a figure had its specific and predetermined square. In the planning of decoration for a chamber, there were rules for which type of scene should go on each wall. The notion of artistic creativity was unknown to the Egyptians and, if suggested, would undoubtedly have horrified them. Excellence in art was excellence in reproducing the traditional design, the function of which was to assist and maintain the tomb occupant in the AFTERLIFE. Departure from the norm was as bad as laying faulty electrical wiring would be today, and an apprentice who sought to vary this would be whipped or dismissed rather than admired.

However, the choice of themes was very wide, from scenes of daily life in the fields and by the river, showing every form of agricultural and rustic activity, to daily life at home and on to battles, processions and feasts. The role of painting as a means of recording rather than of simply celebrating is shown by the literalness of approach. If a VIZIER's retinue consisted of 50 people, then 50 small figures would be depicted in a register, the vizier himself, as befitting his importance, being drawn to a much larger scale in the correct manner. Figures were clearly outlined and painted in the flat, bright colours, with no attempt to suggest shadow. The Egyptians did not discover, or need, perspective as part of their painting technique. The distinctive aspects of Egyptian figure portrayal are very familiar, and perhaps have become less strange to the modern eye during the 20th century, when art sought to break free from the Renaissance tradition. The Egyptian portrait is drawn in profile, but the eye is drawn as if seen full-face. The torso also is facing the viewer, while the waist and legs again are presented in profile. The notion that the Egyptians knew no better is long defunct. Innumerable little figures in hieroglyph, and many SCULPTURES, display their capacity to render a shape with commanding visual realism. There were religious and cultural causes for this form of portrayal, set deep in the mental concrete of the Egyptian sense of tradition. The eye was always a symbol of the first importance, closely identified with HORUS. The artist's duty was to portray each part of the human body in its most 'characteristic' aspect and to combine them into a whole as an assemblage of different elements rather than as a single entity. The major figures are almost always shown in still or seated positions. Painting, especially in the tombs, was for eternity, and the fleeting nature of movement was entirely inappropriate both to the dignity of these figures and to their situation in time. As a result, Egyptian painting has a solemnity in its depiction of large figures that give it a somewhat static appearance. The eye has to look for the many lively details of smaller figures, especially in the painting of animals, where the artist had a freer reign and the capacity for cheerfulness, wit and humour of the Egyptian mind is revealed.

The revolution in religion and political life created by Akhenaten had a profound effect on Egyptian art. The pharaoh demanded realism and the painters struggled to oblige, and the frescoes of the AMARNA PERIOD have a quite different approach, with more vitality and movement than in the old tradition. With the end of the Amarna experiment, the old forms returned but never achieved the distinction of the interrupted tradition. *See also* WRITING.

Artaxerxes I *and* **II** *see* TWENTY-SEVENTH DYNASTY.

Assurbanipal

King of the ASSYRIANS (ruled Egypt 669–640 BC), son of ESARHADDON, who had conquered LOWER EGYPT. The Pharaoh Taharqa retreated far into UPPER EGYPT and provoked rebellion among the northern puppet lords. Esarhaddon died before he could put them down, and Assurbanipal accomplished the task and also marched into Upper Egypt, whereupon Taharqa retreated into NUBIA. Assurbanipal left, only to find his collaborators change sides again. He returned to Egypt and had the DELTA lords and their families executed, sparing only his loyal supporter Necho, lord of SAIS, who was to found the TWENTY-SIXTH DYNASTY. When Taharqa's successor, Tantamani, reinvaded Egypt from Nubia to restore the TWENTY-FIFTH DYNASTY, the Assyrian king's response was swift and overwhelming. He came up the NILE with devastating force, and captured and pillaged Thebes. This put an end to the Twenty-fifth Dynasty, and Assurbanipal again controlled Egypt through the (temporarily) compliant Saites.

Assyrians

One of the major peoples in the Near East in ancient times, with their capital at Nineveh. In 670 BC they invaded Egypt, subdued the DELTA area, and put the whole country under tribute. Unlike the Persians, their kings did not assume the style and dignities of pharaohs, but ruled through Egyptian collaborators. *See also* ASSURBANIPAL, ESARHADDON, TWENTY-SIXTH DYNASTY.

astrology *See* ASTRONOMY.

astronomy
The Egyptians were keen observers of the stars. The book list of the Temple of HORUS at EDFU notes books on such subjects as 'the periodical movement of the sun and moon'. The visible lights in the intensely black night sky were divided into three classes. The Unwearied Stars were the wandering planets: Jupiter, Saturn, Mars, Venus, Mercury. The Imperishable Stars were the circumpolar stars, believed to be the location of heaven. The Indestructible Stars were the fixed stars, of which the Egyptians chose thirty-six to identify the ten-day periods of the CALENDAR year. The constellations were picked out and given names, such as the Hippopotamus and the CROCODILE. The Egyptians did not turn ASTRONOMY into a science, and, like mathematics, it made little progress from the pyramid-building age onwards. They were more concerned with the application of astronomy to everyday life and made no distinction between astronomy and astrology. They believed that every month, day and hour were in the keeping of a particular god who could intervene favourably or unfavourably at the appropriate time. Episodes in the life of the gods fell on certain days, which were labelled as 'good' or 'bad', the bad days noted in texts in red, the colour of SETH. *See also* CALENDAR.

Aswan
Settlement on the NILE and NOME capital, at the first cataract,

now site of the High Dam. The Aswan quarries were the source of a prized red granite. There are important funerary sites nearby

Asyut
Settlement in MIDDLE EGYPT, with large stone quarries nearby. A temple site and NOME capital, whose local deity, the jackal-headed WEPWAWET, became one of the guardians of the Osirian UNDERWORLD.

Atbara
A tributary of the NILE, rising in Ethiopia and joining the main stream at Atbara, north of Khartoum.

Aten *or* Aton
The disc of the sun, its brilliantly visible aspect, as distinct from its mystical, creative aspects, which are linked with AMUN, the 'hidden god'. Aten, on the other hand, was there for all to see and was taken by the AKHENATEN as a universal god. The EIGHTEENTH-DYNASTY cult of Aten was linked to solar cults in neighbouring countries. At this time, numerous temples to Aten were built, to be later demolished. *See also* RA.

Atum
The local god of the DELTA city of HELIOPOLIS, represented in human form and originally seen as creator of the world. The priests of Heliopolis then joined his cult with that of RA, the universal sun-god, with the name of Atum-Ra, during the Second Dynasty. *See also* COSMOLOGY.

Avaris
Site in the eastern DELTA, close to PIRAMESSE, where the HYKSOS kings established their first base before establishing themselves at MEMPHIS.

B

ba
An Egyptian term approximating to 'soul', one of the five elements constituting the human being. The *ba* was present at the weighing of its owner's heart after DEATH, and it was represented as a human-headed bird flying between the two worlds of life and AFTERLIFE.

Badarian Period *see* PRE-DYNASTIC PERIOD.

baking
Baking in the OLD KINGDOM was done in small ovens or by using heated stones. By the ELEVENTH and TWELFTH Dynasties, baking was practised on an almost industrial scale, with large bakeries, often with a brew house attached. Grain brought from the GRANARY was milled by hand, and dough was prepared in vats big enough for the maker to stand in and tread the dough with his feet. Loaves were baked both as flat cakes and in pottery moulds. In such places the arrival of raw material and the output of bread was carefully supervised and recorded, and from such establishments whole estates, or garrisons, would have been supplied.

Bastet
A CAT-headed goddess, guardian of the DELTA area, with her centre of cult at BUBASTIS.

bee

The ancient emblem of LOWER EGYPT, associated with the DELTA town of BUTO.

beer

The staple drink of the common people, taken at any time of day. The Egyptians made beer in various ways. One was to allow lightly baked bread to ferment in water. Another method was based on the use of dates. The end-product was a thickish liquid, low in alcohol but high in food value.

Ben-ben

A truncated OBELISK set on a podium in the temple of the sun-god at HELIOPOLIS, a fetish object representing the sun as creator and also set up in other SUN TEMPLES. This primitive object is the source of much of the symbolism of Egyptian architecture, including the PYRAMIDS.

Beni-Hasan

Capital of the Oryx NOME in UPPER EGYPT, with large limestone deposits and tombs of governors. These rock tombs are among the finest of the MIDDLE KINGDOM period.

bird life

Egypt abounded in bird species, and certain birds play a key part in Egyptian mythology, especially the falcon, identified with HORUS, and the ibis, identified with THOTH. Geese and ducks were the prime domesticated species, kept in large numbers for their eggs and for their fat, flesh and feathers. Cranes were caught in the wild and kept for fattening with the geese. Wild birds were hunted or trapped. Hunters waited eagerly for the winter arrival of migratory species from northern latitudes. Swans and pelicans were known but do not appear to have been numerous as they do not feature in sacrificial offerings. Ostriches, found in the desert, were hunted for their feathers and became very rare.

Blemmyes
A southern desert people, a source of troops for OLD KINGDOM rulers.

Blue Nile
The right-hand branch (looking north) of the NILE, which rises in the mountains of Ethiopia and joins the WHITE NILE at Khartoum.

boat *see* SHIPS AND SHIPBUILDING.

boat pit
Stone-lined pits, often found close to OLD KINGDOM pyramids. Boat pits are either boat-shaped, perhaps to provide the dead king with a sky vessel in which to accompany the sun-god, or rectangular pits containing dismantled wooden BOATS, for the same purpose.

Bocchoris *see* TWENTY-FOURTH DYNASTY.

Book of Caverns
A set of religious illustrations and texts found on the walls of royal tombs of the NEW KINGDOM period. They show the progress of RA through the six caverns of the UNDERWORLD.

Book of the Dead
A collection of NEW KINGDOM and later funerary texts, on PAPYRUS, found in tombs and often placed within the wrappings or between the legs of mummies. Based on the COFFIN TEXTS, which go back to the SIXTH DYNASTY, these writings are spells intended to ease the transition of the dead person into the AFTERWORLD.

There are some ninety 'chapters' altogether, and some versions are very finely written and beautifully illustrated, showing scenes of the dead undergoing judgement, worshipping the gods and at work in the fields of the UNDERWORLD. Some of the texts are written on PAPYRUS rolls up to 120 feet (37 metres) long, whilst others amount to a few scraps. The title, with its portentous ring, is inaccurate, and a better rendition would be the Book of Coming Forth By Day.

Book of Gates

Another work of religious literature from the NEW KINGDOM, found on sarcophagi and tomb walls. It too is a collection of charms and spells to aid the deceased to get past WEPWAWET.

Book of What is in the Underworld

The collective name for a set of funerary texts that originated in the MIDDLE KINGDOM and reached their most definitive form during the NEW KINGDOM reign of AMENOPHIS I. They provide a description of the UNDERWORLD, showing the passage of the sun-god RA through the hours of the night, together with guidance as to the rituals that ensure safe passage into it. Versions of it are found in both royal and private tombs up to the end of the dynastic period.

boomerang

The Egyptians possessed a throwing stick similar to the Australian boomerang and used for the same purposes—hunting and sport.

bronze

This metal, a compound of COPPER and tin, came into use in Egypt during the later MIDDLE KINGDOM, and Egypt remained a

Bubastis

Bronze Age culture even when iron was in extensive use by neighbouring countries.

Bubastis

A religious site in the NILE DELTA, NOME capital and seat of the cult of the CAT-goddess BASTET.

Busiris

A religious site and NOME capital in the DELTA, a focus of the cult of OSIRIS, where a tree was kept as a fetish object, supposedly the tree against which his coffin was washed up. Eventually it was overshadowed by ABYDOS, where the god's heart was said to be buried.

Buto

Patron snake-goddess of LOWER EGYPT, to whom the cobra was sacred. Her original cult centre was the town and NOME capital of the same name, situated on a coastal lagoon in the northern DELTA. She was also called WADJET. Snake-goddesses were usually seen as benign, perhaps because of the snake's useful function of eating rats and other vermin.

Byblos

A port on the Syrian coast, which was used from early times by Egyptian sailors, and where numerous ancient Egyptian relics have been discovered. In the OSIRIS legend, his coffin chest was washed ashore there.

C

calendar

From a very early time, the Egyptians had a form of calendar based on the phases of the moon. From around the end of the Second Dynasty (2700 BC), they developed a more accurate calendar that divided the year into 365 days. Their new year began with the arrival of the INUNDATION at MEMPHIS, and was more precisely marked by the heliacal rising of the bright star Sirius (SOTHIS). It was divided into three seasons, each of four months lasting thirty days. There were five 'extra' days, designated as feast days and spread throughout the year. As they made no provision for a leap year, the calendar and the seasons drifted out of step, and by the end of the OLD KINGDOM there was a discrepancy of five months.

The invention of the calendar has been seen as one of the great Egyptian contributions to human knowledge. *See also* ASTRONOMY.

canals

Canals were relatively easy to dig in the alluvial soil of the NILE Valley and DELTA, but the Egyptians also attempted to cut canals through more intractable country, including the first cataract of the Nile, where evidence can still be seen of their effort to cut a channel through the rock. Sesostris III, in the MIDDLE KINGDOM, was able to proceed by BOAT all the way to the second cataract on his expedition to push back the Nubians. The most ambitious

canal venture was the attempt made by the TWENTY-SIXTH-DY-
NASTY king, Necho II, to cut a waterway from the Mediterranean
Sea, via the Damietta branch of the Nile, to the Red Sea, antici-
pating the Suez Canal by some 2,500 years. This work was completed under the Persian suzerainty of DARIUS I.

Cambyses *see* TWENTY-SEVENTH DYNASTY.

canopic jar
A jar sealed with a mud-paste cap in the OLD KINGDOM and with
a cap carved like a human head in the MIDDLE KINGDOM, and with
the heads of the four sons of HORUS in the later NEW KINGDOM.
Four jars were used for preserving the entrails of the mummified
dead. It was apparently so called from the town of Canopus, on
the sea coast of the DELTA, but this is a modern connection without historical verification.

capitals
Egyptian COLUMNS had two distinctive types of capital, whether
carved or decorated. One is known as the bud-form or bell-form
capital, based on the lotus bud, and the other the spreading capital, based on the open lotus flower. These two types can be seen
clearly in the design of the HYPOSTYLE HALL at KARNAK, where the
'master' columns are of the open form and the 'minor' ones of
the closed form. *See also* ARCHITECTURE, COLUMN, TEMPLE.

Carnarvon, Lord
(1866–1923) British aristocrat and passionate amateur Egyptologist, who sponsored the excavations of Howard CARTER at THEBES,
which led to the discovery of the tomb of TUTANKHAMUN.

carpentry
In the PRE-DYNASTIC and THINITE PERIODS, there may still have

been woodlands with hardwood trees, but whether the timber used was native or imported, Egyptian woodworking reached a very high standard at an early stage. Wood was cut, jointed, shaped, inlaid and polished with techniques and results that rival anything achieved since. The Egyptians mastered the principle of concealed joints and could manufacture a form of plywood. A full range of household furniture was produced, from doors to beds, stools, tables and chests, as well as smaller wooden items like game boards. Many of the carpenter's implements were made of stone; the plane, for example, was not known and surfaces were levelled and smoothed with polishing stones. Axes, adzes and chisels, of stone or COPPER, were the main tools. Copper saws came into use during the early dynastic period, including large pull saws. Hand drills with FLINT blades were widely used. *See also* SHIPS AND SHIPBUILDING.

Carter, Howard
(1874–1939) British Egyptologist, who discovered the tomb of TUTANKHAMUN, with its treasures still intact, in 1922. He also found the tombs of HATSHEPSUT and Tuthmosis IV.

cartouche
Around the start of the THIRD DYNASTY, the practice arose of enclosing a king's name, and sometimes his whole set of ceremonial titles, in a cartouche, or drawn oval frame, set on a square base. To the Egyptians, this oval represented the elliptical course of the sun around the world and defined the limits of the kingdom that it lit.

cat
Cat cemeteries have been found at BUBASTIS in the DELTA and at

cataracts

Beni Hasan in UPPER EGYPT, where mummified cats were buried in very large numbers. These localities had CAT temples, and regarded the animals as sacred. *See also* ANIMAL CULTS.

cataracts

Sections of the River NILE where there are rapids and waterfalls created by hard bands of granitic rock and making obstructions to easy transport on the river. There were six sets of CATARACTS, stretching upriver from ASWAN, at the Nubian border, far into what is now SUDAN.

Champollion, Jean-François

(1790–1832) French Egyptologist, who first analysed the hieroglyphic script of ancient Egypt in an epoch-making lecture to the Académie Française on 22 September 1822. His further work was published as *Monuments d'Egypte et Nubie*, and a *Grammaire Egyptien*, which was published posthumously in 1835.

chancellor

The Controller of the Seal—a very senior official of the royal court, whose responsibilities included tax levying and collection, and being paymaster general to the ARMY and navy. The two treasuries, the White House of UPPER EGYPT and the Red House of LOWER EGYPT, were under his supervision. At times both Lower and Upper Egypt would have separate chancellors. *See also* ECONOMY, TRADE.

chemistry

The derivation of the word has been traced by some back to the *khemet*, or 'black land', of Egypt. Drugs and ointments were prepared for all manner of purposes, from anointing statues to sweetening breath. The Egyptians also refined and combined precious metals, developing processes for enamelling, gilding and casting.

Cheops *or* Khufu

A PHARAOH of the FOURTH DYNASTY (between 2625 and 2510 BC) for whom the Great Pyramid at GIZA was constructed.

Chephren *or* Khephren

A PHARAOH of the FOURTH DYNASTY (between 2625 and 2510 BC) whose PYRAMID is found close to that of CHEOPS, at GIZA. Chephren also had the Great SPHINX carved, as a guardian figure for his funerary site.

children

There were many worse places to be a child than in ancient Egypt. The normal tenor of life was calm and peaceful, the DIET was usually varied and adequate, the climate encouraged a life out of doors, in the shade of a reed awning by a hut or the shady inner courtyard of a house with its tree-lined pool. The Egyptians were kind to their children, and in their society there were none of the rites of mutilation or ordeal that among many communities marked the passage into the adult world. Although boys enjoyed more status than girls, the Egyptians did not practise the killing of unwanted female children by exposure. Childhood was short, however. Puberty came early and a girl might be married and have her first child by the age of 12 or 13. By the age of 16, a boy came officially into manhood and could hold administrative and priestly positions. *See also* EDUCATION.

childbirth

Since all recorded contemporary evidence from ancient Egypt is produced by men, the information on childbirth is scanty. Births took place within the family home, with the assistance of a midwife. A birthing stool was used for the mother to squat on, her baby passing through a hole in the seat into the hands of the midwife. The umbilical cord was cut with a knife of obsidian, and the placenta was sometimes buried at the doorstep but sometimes may also have been eaten, or partly eaten, by the mother.

chronology

Working out the time scale of ancient Egypt is a complex business. Our numbering of PHARAOHS as AMENOPHIS I or TUTHMOSIS I, II, and so on, was not practised by the Egyptians, who gave each of their kings a full and distinctive set of names. Egyptian scripts number the years from the start of the current king's reign, but we know nothing about their birth dates or the length of most reigns and so cannot simply use the kings' lives to count back to some original starting point. For early Egyptologists, the evidence of texts, combined with (for the LATE PERIOD) cross-references to the Bible, were the prime means of dating events in ancient Egypt. More recently, the contents of RUBBISH MOUNDS have been studied as closely as tomb walls. The scientific dating techniques of modern archaeology, based on measuring river erosion and deposits, on aerial photography, including infrared photography, and measuring the age of artefacts through radiocarbon dating and potassium-argon dating, have brought much greater precision into this area, but there are still uncertainties.

circumcision

Male circumcision was practised throughout the OLD and MIDDLE KINGDOM periods, not in babyhood but between the ages of six and twelve. HERODOTUS reported that it was done for reasons of hygiene. There is no textual evidence of female circumcision, and no circumcised female mummies have been found.

cities

Ancient Egypt possessed no cities in the sense of great metropolitan centres with a mass of population, with the possible exception of THEBES and MEMPHIS, until the rise of ALEXANDRIA under Greek rule. The population was distributed throughout the long, narrow country, reflecting the agricultural basis of Egyptian life. The largest towns were the royal capitals like Memphis and Thebes, or major cult centres like HELIOPOLIS. But their growth was limited by the lack of transport other than river transport, the perishability of produce and the availability of good water. In the hot CLIMATE of Egypt, the close-packed network of narrow town streets, with the ubiquitous rubbish heaps picked over by dogs, donkeys and rats, must often have been smelly and unsalubrious.

Cleopatra

(69–30 BC) The last independent ruler of ancient Egypt (ruled 51–30 BC). She was not an Egyptian but a Greek, descended from Ptolemy Lago, the first Greek emperor. By her father's will she should have shared the throne with her brother but was ousted by his supporters. By this time Egypt had come within the sphere of influence of pre-Imperial Rome, and the dictator Julius Caesar took Cleopatra's side and restored her to the throne. She bore Caesar a son, Cesarion. Later she became the lover of Mark Antony and sided with him against Octavius, who defeated them at the naval battle of Actium. Cleopatra opened negotiations with Octavius (Emperor Augustus) but to no avail, and, after learning of Mark Antony's suicide, she took her own life. Egypt became a colony of Rome, as a fief of the emperor. *See also* PTOLEMAIC DYNASTY.

climate

The climate of Egypt is generally hot and dry. The DELTA area, influenced by the Mediterranean Sea, has a mean summer temperature in the 25–35°C band, whilst in the NILE Valley proper, with arid desert on each side, it rises to 40°C and more. The days are typically clear and cloudless. As in all subtropical desert climates, nights can be cold, even below freezing in exposed regions. A beneficial aspect of the desert winds was that even in the marshy areas of the Delta and the Valley, malaria was unknown.

coffin texts

Funerary inscriptions made on sarcophagi, usually formulae forming part of the ritual established to ensure that the spirit of the deceased passed successfully through to the AFTERWORLD. These date from the SIXTH DYNASTY, later than the PYRAMID TEXTS, and they are found not only on the tombs of kings, indicating that by this time knowledge of the precious, secret spells had spread to a wider, if still aristocratic, group. There are over 1,000 spells recorded. *See also* BOOK OF THE DEAD.

colossal statues

The origin of the vastly larger than life statues of PHARAOHS can be traced to their semi-godlike status and the political cult of kingship that made the most of this traditional view for the benefit of the ruling dynasty. Something comparable can be seen also in the 'perspective' of Egyptian painting, which accords greater stature to the most important personages depicted. This sense of scale based on status, together with the serenity exhibited by the colossal statues such as those of RAMESES II, prevent these superhuman sculptures from seeming completely megalomaniac in purpose and expression. Most statues were, if anything, smaller than life size.

Colossi of Memnon

Two COLOSSAL STATUES carved in the reign of AMENOPHIS III (EIGHT-EENTH DYNASTY) as guardian figures to his MORTUARY TEMPLE at Malkata on the west bank of the NILE, at THEBES. The Greeks confused, or assimilated, Amenophis with their mythical hero Memnon, who figures in the *Iliad*, and believed that Memnon was buried there. An earthquake in 27 BC opened cracks in the stone, in which dew formed during the chilly night. With the heat of day the moisture evaporated and expanded, creating a moaning sound that impressed the superstitious Greeks. The moaning stopped when the Roman Emperor Septimius Severus had the monuments repaired.

columns

These were vital features of Egyptian ARCHITECTURE, essential for any building of size in order to support the weight of a roof or upper storey. Columns cut in the rock tombs of BENI-HASAN have some-times been taken to prefigure the Greek Doric column. Their faces have been planed to present first eight, then sixteen facets, and the facets have been hollowed out to give extra effect to the edges. Doric columns were still 2,000 years in the future, but in the LATE PERIOD the Greeks were close observers of Egyptian detail. The standard Egyptian column decreases slightly in girth from base to top, sits on a plain flat stone base, and it terminates in an abacus, or square slab, of the same width as the beam that it supports (a feature unusual in later columnar structures). The great columns of KARNAK are 60 feet (18 metres) high and 12 feet (4 metres) in diameter; the blocks they support are 36 feet (11 metres) long and 4 feet (122 centimetres) thick. There is no contemporary indication of how these structures could be erected, but one theory is that the temple building was

concubinage

filled with earth, or sandbags, so that the working floor rose as the columns rose, with the great blocks gradually raised to the working level by wedges. *See also* TEMPLE.

concubinage

In addition to a chief wife and a number of subordinate wives, a wealthy man might have a number of concubines, in circumstances similar to the harem of later, Ottoman times. Although of lower status than the official wives, the concubines might have considerable power in the harem, and there are examples of concubines' sons who attained the kingship.

conception and contraception

On the whole, the Egyptians sought to have large families, partly because of the high infant mortality rate, which meant that only a few would survive, partly because a numerous progeny reflected credit on both parents, but perhaps especially the father. Fertility, the gift of OSIRIS, was prized, and sterility, by the same token, was considered more than unfortunate. A childless wife (the wife was invariably held responsible) was likely to be returned to her father. There were many more nostrums and prescriptions for aiding conception than for preventing it, and the Egyptians also developed their own forms of pregnancy tests to confirm the good news. Potency was regarded as necessary for full enjoyment of the AFTERLIFE as well as the present. Nevertheless, contraception was also practised, although the measures prescribed were more bizarre than efficacious, being based on magic rather than science, with considerable use of CROCODILE droppings.

copper

The principal metal used by the Egyptians. Copper was mined on the SINAI PENINSULA but in quite small quantities. Known from the beginning of the PRE-DYNASTIC PERIOD, it remained in short supply and was seen as a precious metal, but by the time of the pyramid-builders, it was common enough to be used for tools, although probably only the wealthiest or most talented of masons had copper chisels. Copper was used by sculptors in the SIXTH DYNASTY, from which we have a fine copper statue of PEPY I.

Coptic

The language of the Egyptian Christians, in diminishing daily use until the 18th century and still preserved as a liturgical language. It has much altered elements of Egyptian, heavily admixed with ancient Greek, but was invaluable to the 19th-century Egyptologists in their efforts to decode the hieroglyphic script. *See also* CHAMPOLLION; LANGUAGE.

cosmetics

Cosmetics were important both for decorative and for hygienic reasons. The Egyptians were especially concerned with emphasising the eyes, and kohl, made from the mineral galena, was used to lengthen the eyebrows and darken the eyelids, and to extend the outer corners of the eyes. It was used in powder form and applied with the finger or a flat instrument. Red ochre was used as rouge, and henna as a lightening dye for hair and nails. Scented oils and ointments were widely used. These were made and blended from a variety of ingredients, including almond oil, cinnamon, cardamoms, honey, olive oil, frankincense and myrrh, many of these imported down-river from NUBIA and Ethiopia as raw materials and refined and blended in Egyptian workshops. More basic pastes would also be made to help protect the skin of people who were obliged to work all day in the fields; it is un-

cosmology

likely that the Egyptians indulged in sunbathing. Cosmetics were
used by both men and women. *See also* ORNAMENTATION.

cosmology
The ancient Egyptians' attitude to the heavens was not exploratory or analytical. They observed the patterns of the stars, moon
and sun closely, and from the earliest times had framed legends
and descriptions that sought to give the remote and unattainable
sky some earthly parallels. Since the sky must have some support, they endowed it with four great pillars. These were seen
sometimes as the legs of a cow, along the line of whose belly the
sun travelled; sometimes as the arms and legs of the sky-goddess, NUT, whose naked form arched across the sky. The ancient
Egyptian cosmologies, efforts to explain the source of the world,
all start from the two immemorial aspects of life in Egypt—the
annual flooding of the NILE, and the almost perpetual brilliance
throughout the day of the sun. The first Egyptian cosmology is
that of HELIOPOLIS, an ancient cult centre. In the beginning was
the wild watery chaos called NUN, and from this the sun emerged,
self-formed. He appeared on earth at Heliopolis in the form of a
stone (the BEN-BEN stone was kept as a cult object in the temple
there). This god was known as RA ('sun') or ATUM ('perfect being'). By the act of masturbation, Ra created from his own seed
the god of air and dryness, SHU, and the goddess of wet, Tefnut.
From their union came the god of earth, GEB, and the sky goddess, Nut. These in turn had four children, OSIRIS, ISIS, SETH and
NEPHTHYS. These nine are known as the Great Ennead. Seth and
Nephthys had no offspring, but Osiris and Isis were fertile.

The second great cosmology was that of Hermopolis (modern
Ashmunein), a NOME capital of UPPER EGYPT about 210 miles (338

kilometres) south of Cairo. Again starting with a formless expanse of water, it endowed the water itself with creative power. Summoned by THOTH, the diety of Hermopolis, and at that very site, it brought forth four frogs and four serpents, which in combination produced an egg that they set upon a mound emerging from the water. From this egg was hatched the sun. The eight creatures formed an OGDOAD, a number of significance to the Egyptians. They were Nun (as in the Heliopolitan system) and his consort, Nunet, Heh and Hehet, flowing water, Keku and Keket, darkness, and AMUN and his consort, Amaunet, light.

Both the Heliopolitan and the Hermopolitan myths have ancient roots that reach far back into primitive and prehistoric African cultures. The third Egyptian cosmology is of a different sort. During the SECOND DYNASTY, when the rulers were based at MEMPHIS, a major effort was made to establish the local Memphite god, PTAH, as a major deity who should command the veneration of all the Egyptians. The Doctrine of Memphis asserted that Ptah was older than ATUM, coeval with the waters from which Atum emerged, and that he created Atum-Ra by a process of pure thought. This was an entirely political move, theologically unnecessary, and intended to supplant the supremacy of Heliopolis and Hermopolis. This cult of Ptah did not survive the THINITE PERIOD, though he remained a significant deity, patron especially of artists and writers, as suited his unusually abstract and intellectual theology. *See also* GODS, RELIGION, THEOLOGY.

costume

The Egyptians had mastered the art of spinning cloth by the beginning of the dynastic period. Since they lived in a country that was almost always warm and often very hot, they did not need heavy garments. The basic garment was simply a loin cloth, worn originally by aristocrat and peasant alike, and many pictures suggest that nudity was not uncommon (although an observer of western art might make the same deduction, falsely). In the dynastic period, this evolved into a kilt-like garment for the nobility, whilst the great majority of the population continued to wear the loin cloth. For ceremonial occasions, priests or nobles wore a long robe, made of a single piece of cloth and reaching from the shoulder to the calf. From the MIDDLE KINGDOM on, they wore beneath it a close-fitting tunic. Women wore a more close-fitting robe that reached to the ankles. Very young CHILDREN wore no clothes; older children wore a version of adult costume. Linen was the prime dressmaking material; the Egyptians had been making it since the PRE-DYNASTIC PERIOD and brought its manufacture to a high art. Good clothes were expensive, ranking high in the barter system, and were often subject to theft. White was always the colour of formal clothing, and the Egyptians either did not master, or did not care to use, the techniques of dyeing linen. Instead they developed elaborate forms of pleating to display the quality of fine cloth. Personal ORNAMENTATION was important. This included wigs, as the heads, of men at least, were normally closely shaven during the OLD KINGDOM and later. Leatherwork was often very fine, with leather being used for sandals and belts, as well as being beaten and rolled out to provide a writing surface. Many people, however, went barefoot some or all of the time.

court life

The court of a PHARAOH had many aspects, because every part of the country's life was here gathered into a single complex system and ultimately into a single personage, the pharaoh, the venerated god-king whose word was more than law, it was divine truth. The life of the court was stately and cermonious, with a number of religious services on each day and a procedure that, although in any one reign it may have seemed inflexible and unchanging, nevertheless evolved gradually as the dynasties passed, without, however, altering in its fundamental principles. The palace and its decorations and feasts were splendid and designed to overawe. Even although the pharaoh himself might be an ascetic, he lived in external magnificence in order to dramatize his difference to even the greatest of the nobility. The palace required a large staff to work effectively, but many of its higher functionaries were decorative, to provide society for the pharaoh and to add lustre to his retinue as he proceeded from place to place. The pharaohs divided their time between the two lands, with a residence in both LOWER and UPPER EGYPT, and the household was frequently on the move. Closest to the king, apart from his immediate family, were the HONOURED ONES, a circle of eminent advisers. Within this group some were awarded special titles of distinction, such as Unique Friend (*see* WENI). In the fixed hierarchical structure of the court, these titles were eagerly sought. Others bore titles of office, chief among them being the VIZIER, although his responsibilities were external rather than within the household. A formidable array of officials controlled all aspects of the PHARAOH'S DAY. His crown and jewels were looked after by the Lord of the Secret of the Royal House; his dress and ornamentation by the Director of the King's Dress, who in turn had a set of officials responsible for individual parts, like wigs, oils and footwear. The libraries, the kitchens, the gardens, all had their own hierarchy within the greater hierarchy. Each task, whether it was the washing of the pharaoh's hands or the tying of his shoes, must be performed by the appropriate functionary. The principal non-religious event of the day was the audience with the vizier, who reported on all matters relating to the administration of the kingdom. Each event was in charge of a master of protocol, whose business it was to see that tradition was not upset. In theory the king, as fountain of justice, was accessible to all his people, and his was the ultimate court of appeal. He alone could confirm a sentence of death.

The queen, the lesser queens and the royal harem had a staff of their own, just as elaborate as the king's but focused on the internal affairs of the women's quarters and the public role of the queens as consorts in attendance on all state occasions.

Despite the weight of protocol and tradition, there was scope for promotion within the ranks of the courtiers. Intelligence was useful, so long as it was not linked to subversiveness or excessive originality of mind. The ponderous framework of court life required a great deal of management and resourcefulness in crisis. An able courtier of fairly low beginnings might be given a number of tasks at different times, from leading a QUARRYING expedition and ensuring safe delivery of the stone to sitting in judgement on disputes among his peers or supervising a group of royal estates, or even acting as a general on a military raid. If he performed satisfactorily and showed himself to be thoroughly and utterly the king's man in every aspect of his life, he might end up as a Unique Friend, with his own royally provided tomb set in proximity to the ruler's own, so that in the AFTERLIFE he might continue to serve with the same devotion.

crime and punishment

The need for civil order was instilled in the Egyptian consciousness from the very earliest times. The whole system of irrigation and cultivation required cooperation and harmony, and anything that disturbed the balance was deplored. Most crime was of a petty nature, punished by fines or by beating. Imprisonment was also used during the MIDDLE KINGDOM to punish those who evaded the annual forced labour. More serious crimes would be punished by mutilation or the infliction of a set number of wounds. No doubt these often led to death, but the death sentence itself was extremely rare in ancient Egypt. The most heinous crime was tomb robbing, which is by no means a modern activity. Its origins are almost as old as the practice of depositing valuable objects in the tomb, and all the Egyptians' reverence for the gods and the spirits of the departed did not deter tomb robbing. It was especially common in times of hardship and famine, and during the TWENTIETH and TWENTY-FIRST Dynasties it became an epidemic, and horrified priests were reduced to gathering up despoiled mummies and bundling them into secret caves. One such was discovered in the cliffs of the VALLEY OF THE KINGS in 1881—there were 36 mummies piled in it. A TOMB ROBBER, if caught, could expect to have his ears and nose slit and to be impaled through the rectum on a pole.

Criosphinx
A ram-headed SPHINX.

crocodile
This reptile lived in the NILE in substantial numbers, and the Egyptians treated it with great respect. One of the NOMES was called the Crocodile NOME. The god SETH was sometimes represented in crocodile form. But the crocodile is chiefly associated with the god SEBEK, who had a crocodile head, with a cult cen-

crown

tre at Crocodilopolis in the FAIYUM (Greek: 'crocodile city'), set up in the course of the MIDDLE KINGDOM. Sacred crocodiles were kept here, and preserved in a crocodile NECROPOLIS.

crown

The crown was an important part of the royal REGALIA, with strong symbolic value expressing the dualism and unity of the Egyptian kingdom. There were two crowns, the Red Crown of LOWER EGYPT and the White Crown of UPPER EGYPT, the colours corresponding to other things emblematic of the original division. They could be worn separately or combined in a single crown, the Double Crown.

cubit

A linear unit of MEASUREMENT. The Egyptian standard cubit was approximately 18 inches (46 centimetres), although there was also the royal cubit of approximately 20 inches (51 centimetres).

currency

Coinage was not used in ancient Egypt until the First Persian Occupation. *See also* TRADE, WEIGHTS AND MEASURES.

D

Dahshur

An important funerary site in the MEMPHIS area, on the west bank of the NILE, just south of SAQQARA. It has two PYRAMIDS built by SNOFRU (FIFTH DYNASTY), and the TWELFTH DYNASTY pyramids of Ammenemes II, Sesostris III and Ammenemes III, who had another about, 50 miles (80 kilometres) farther south, at Hawara.

Darius I

King of the Persians and suzerain of Egypt (548–486 BC). During his reign coinage was introduced to Egypt. He visited Egypt to put down uprisings and completed the NILE-Red Sea CANAL. Darius also built temples in Egypt, re-opening the quarries at Wadi Hammamet in order to build a temple to AMUN-RA at the nearby el-Kargha oasis, and under his rule Egypt appears to have prospered.

Darius II *see* TWENTY-SEVENTH DYNASTY.

death

The Egyptian attitude to death has fascinated every succeeding generation. So much of peoples' lives and energy in that sunlit, fertile land, so favoured by nature, was devoted to preparation for death and to the maintenance of entire towns of the dead, that the Egyptians were viewed as a morbid, gloomy, death-obsessed nation, stuck in a cul-de-sac of human thought and cosmological speculation. Yet there is ample evidence that the Egyptians were a cheerful people who appreciated and enjoyed the natural advantages their country possessed and who had time for the same celebrations and enjoyments of life as any other people, from harvest feasts to board games and dirty jokes. In a paradoxical way, their preoccupation with death may have stemmed from their enjoyment of life. Their awareness of life was exceptionally vivid and strong, not merely in the sense of being alive but in their perception of the sun-driven life force that animates the whole of nature. They were lovers of life, and because they loved it so much, life seemed all too brief. Just as they believed that certain creatures were born spontaneously from mud, created by the life force, so they also felt that the life force within themselves was not spent and exhausted on death; it carried on but in another form. Since they knew that life was short, and death was long, it seemed entirely reasonable to treat the brief period of life as the opportunity to prepare their long homes, where their spirits would reside for eternity.

The *KA*, or life force, was not the only element to constitute the human being. The Egyptians also distinguished the *AKH*, the link between the living person and the sun; the *HA*, an unbodied, independent entity that emanated from the power of its owner and was independent of the body (unlike the *ka*, which needed some physical form); and finally the name, which had a magic definitive power of its own that continued to identify the individual even after the body had disintegrated. All these attributes survived and had to be provided for in the tomb. *See also* AFTERLIFE, UNDERWORLD.

deben

From the Ramessid time onwards, a standard weight, equivalent to about 3¹/₄ ounces (91 grams), used for expressing values in trade. There was a COPPER, SILVER and GOLD deben, in ascending order of value. *See also* MEASUREMENT.

Delta

The great fan-shaped area of marshland intersected by waterways, over 100 miles (161 kilometres) long, between the two great arms into which the NILE divides north of MEMPHIS before it eventually meets the sea. The Delta (so called from its resemblance to the triangular shape of the Greek letter 'd') has been created through millennia by the soil and grit brought down by the river. As the river's speed drops, it can move less and less of this material, which sinks to the river floor, and so the delta is gradually formed. Apart from the richness of the soil, the region offered protection from overland raiding and ample building material in the form of the tall reeds used both for house and shipbuilding. It was in the Delta area that Egyptian civilization began, but the annual deposit of new soil means that the earliest relics of life there are now far below ground level. *See also* SHIPS AND SHIPBUILDING.

Deir el Bahri

The site of the EIGHTEENTH DYNASTY tomb of Queen HATSHEPSUT, and the PYRAMID and temple of Mentuhotpe, in the hills of the west bank of the NILE, opposite THEBES.

Deir el Medina

Dating from the Ramessid period, this is the site, a short distance south of DEIR EL BAHRI, of a well-preserved workmen's village for 120 artisans and their families. In the ELEVENTH DYNASTY it was a cemetery area, an extension of Deir el Bahri. When the VALLEY OF THE KINGS came into use as a place of burial, the village was set up, in the reign of TUTHMOSIS I. Its peak of activity was during the NINETEENTH and TWENTIETH DYNASTIES, but activity continued until the TWENTY-FIFTH DYNASTY, when a chapel to OSIRIS was erected. The site is of particular interest in what it reveals of the daily lives of skilled artisans and craftsmen, who lived there and worked on the royal sites in ten-day shifts, with one day off. They included scribes, draughtsmen, sculptors, wood-carvers, plasterers, masons and stucco-workers, mostly Egyptian but with a leavening of foreigners from NUBIA, Syria and LIBYA. The village was aligned on a north-south axis, with a guarded gate at each end and a central roadway. The houses, set close to each other without gardens, were built of rough stone up to the 5-foot (1.5-metre) line, and then of mud brick, with mud plaster on a framework of wooden laths for a roof. The walls were painted white, the doors red. The front room had an altar built into the wall, for domestic rituals relating to ancestor cult and such deities as Bes, the god of fertility and CHILD-BIRTH. The second room, larger and higher, was supported by a column, and its main piece of furniture was a couch. These were the 'public' rooms, with the family living quarters behind and a small subterranean storage room. The kitchen gave access to further cellar space and to the roof, which was substantial enough to be used as a terrace for relaxation in the evening. The kitchen had an oven, grindstones, mortars and jars, with stone knives and other implements. There was no water supply, no drainage, and water came by donkey from the nearest wells.

Adjoining the village at the north end are small cult chapels, each with space for a meeting room, then a little anteroom to the sanctuary and the sanctuary itself with a god's statue. Among the cults were those of HATHOR, AMUN and AMENOPHIS I. The workers had their own cemetery, with family tombs formed by an arched chamber of mud bricks. Later these were given a PYRAMID shape, which would have been seen as sacrilegious in the OLD KING-DOM. The tomb itself was underground, with a mortuary chapel above it. As far as they could, the workers reproduced the decoration, furniture and ornament of the royal tombs where they worked in the more modest tombs they built for themselves.

Provisions came from the store rooms of temples in the neighbourhood, and if these were inadequate, the workmen were liable to go on strike. Social life within the little community was introspective, and the records indicate a characteristic litany of minor crimes, adulteries and disturbances that suggest something other, and more normal, than a dedicated community where all is industry and harmony.

demotic

A speeded-up form of writing Egyptian (from Greek *demo-tikos*, 'popular'), introduced some 200 years after HIERATIC. Its characters are cursive and flowing, and far removed from the original pictorial basis of HIEROGLYPHICS.

Den

A First-Dynasty king (ruled 3050–2995 BC), the first to be given the title 'he who belongs to the SEDGE and the BEE' (symbols of UPPER and LOWER EGYPT respectively). He was the first king to add a third name to his titulature. This was known as the *nsw-bty* name, or 'king of Upper and Lower Egypt' name, intended to emphasize his role as monarch of the entire country. *See also* FIRST AND SECOND DYNASTIES.

Dendera

The site in UPPER EGYPT, close to EDFU, of a major temple of the

57

dendrochronology

goddess HATHOR. A yearly festival linked the two sites, bringing the image of Hathor to Edfu to re-enact the conception of the young HORUS.

dendrochronology
The science of dating timber and wooden structures.

dentistry
Dentistry, in as far as it existed,was a department of medicine, not a separate science. The Egyptians' DIET, sugar-free and with quite a high fibrous content, was not injurious to the enamel of the teeth, and the dental problems that feature among the admittedly very sparse medical records left to us are more concerned with loose and missing teeth. The major dental problems were worn-down teeth and dental abscesses; few Egyptians can have avoided the pain of toothache. It is likely that the Egyptians cleaned their teeth with narrow 'brushes' made of fibry wood, or toothpicks, possibly with a paste whose aim would have been to sweeten the breath rather than to offer dental protection.

diet
The Egyptians ate a single daily main meal at sunset. For the well-off, the diet was varied, with game of many sorts, such as the antelope, ibex and gazelle, and wild fowl from swamp or desert, although the staple meats were the farm-kept geese, beef, goat and mutton. Pork was regarded as unclean, with the pig placed in the realm of SETH. The rich also ate very little in the way of fish, which was also considered an unclean food, probably because of its rapid propensity to spoil. Among their vegetables were onions, leeks, garlic, beans, peas, lentils, carrots, turnips, spinach and radishes. Figs, dates, grapes and pomegran-

ates were the principal fruits. Dried sea salt from the DELTA coast was shipped throughout the country, and there were rock-salt deposits also. Spices were widely used, then as now. Bread was baked in ovens or using specially heated flat stones. The diet of the peasants and serfs was less varied, with grains and pulses playing a major part, but they also ate fish without compunction.

disease

The Egyptians were likely to meet their deaths through disease or the complications of disease rather than in any other way. Smallpox, leprosy and poliomyelitis were all uncurable killer diseases. Rheumatism and arthritis were common. The most common sexually transmitted disease was gonorrhea. Bilharzia and other waterborne diseases were passed on through contaminated NILE water, since all sorts of refuse, from the towns of NUBIA down, went into the river. Cuts, wounds and scrapes had a high likelihood of leading to sepsis and gangrene. *See also* MEDICINE.

divorce *see* MARRIAGE CUSTOMS.

Djadjat

A local council of elders and notables, advisers to the provincial governor as part of the LEGAL SYSTEM.

Djer *see* FIRST AND SECOND DYNASTIES.

Djoser *or* **Zoser** *see* THIRD DYNASTY.

drink

The Egyptians brewed BEER in various forms, notably by allowing specially made, part-cooked loaves of barley or wheat to ferment in water, and this formed the staple drink of the great mass of the people. Wine production, both red and white, goes back to the ori-

dromos

gins of the OLD KINGDOM, and perhaps the PRE-DYNASTIC PERIOD, but the cost of production always made it a luxury item for the wealthy few. There were wine connoisseurs who appreciated a good wine and knew the best places to obtain it, although Egyptian wine contained resins for preservative or flavouring purposes

dromos

A processional way leading up to the entrance of a TEMPLE.

dualism

Egypt was formed from two kingdoms, and this fact was never forgotten. It became firmly imprinted on life and culture. The king wore the emblems of both, the BEE of LOWER EGYPT, and the lily (SEDGE) of UPPER EGYPT. The national institutions were duplicated, with a TREASURY (the Red House) for Lower Egypt, and another, the White House, for Upper Egypt. Similarly, each possessed a GRANARY, and the king had a palace in each. Kings from the THINITE PERIOD onwards usually had tombs built in each part of the country. The concept of opposites linked in a harmonious unity is also basic to much of Egyptian thought, as the story of OSIRIS and SETH shows. Such dualism does not imply an equal balance in the Egyptian mind. Horus would always triumph over Seth.

dynasty

A royal house, or a sequence of rulers, the successive families who inherited or took over the kingship. There were 30 dynasties, varying greatly in length, and some of them existing simultaneously with another. The reasons for separating the different dynasties are not always clear, and often there was at least some hereditary continuation from one to the next. Equally, there appear to be complete breaks of hereditary succession within certain dynasties. Location played a part, as the centre of power shifted up and down the NILE Valley. The dynasty lists have been handed down from the compilation of MANETHO and other contemporary sources, and as the science of Egyptology progresses, it may be that they will be discarded or revised as more accurate means of tracing the ruling families become available. *See individual entries.*

E

Early Pre-dynastic Period *see* PRE-DYNASTIC PERIOD.

economy

Egypt, especially in the formative period of the unitary state, was organized as a despotism. The king was all-powerful and, with a small group of his relatives and chosen administrators, imposed his will on every aspect of the people's lives. The entire country, its wealth and its population was his. His vast power was limited by the general respect for justice and the law, already a matter of ancient tradition, and religion, a matter of even more ancient tradition; and by the enduring political configuration of the country—the two Egypts, the NOMES, the regional and provincial loyalties of the population. Unlike later despots, the pharaoh did not have a large standing ARMY at his disposal, but he did have on his side custom, tradition and a more than earthly prestige. He was also owner of great estates in his own right, and of even more as high priest, since the temples came to be the second-greatest landowner after the crown, and also any unallocated or conquered land was in his gift. He controlled imports, exports, mining, quarrying and metalworking, and he levied taxes. Taxation was the responsibility of an official known as the CHANCELLOR, a deputy of the VIZIER, whose court title was Controller of the Seal, and he had two great central TREASURIES or storehouses, the Red Treasury of LOWER EGYPT, in the DELTA, and the White Treasury of UPPER EGYPT, at MEMPHIS. In a country with no coinage, taxation was a matter of payment in kind. The fiscal storehouses were extraordinary places that took in every kind of produce and manufactured article, although corn, dates, flour and hides must have formed the great bulk of it. A substantial and efficient distribution network was necessary in order to redistribute this hoard of goods, often perishable, to the court, the temples, the tomb cities and other recipients of the king's largesse. The chancellor and his staff computed the tax levels using a number of different criteria. By far the most important among these were the level of the last INUNDATION and the consequent agricultural yield that could be anticipated—an over-generous flood could be as disastrous as a meagre one. The chancellor's taxes had also to be enough to finance whatever plans the king might have, whether a foreign expedition or a PYRAMID to excel all others; and, as many projects lasted for many years, he had to think far ahead. He was aided by a well-established system of inspections and censuses, the Egyptian passion for making lists proving useful in such connections. His department needed extensive records, since many temples and funerary estates had tax privileges of one kind or another (*see* LAND OWNERSHIP).

Since the court, the government and the state were an indissolubly single entity, the government could never go bankrupt. Except in times of emergency, economic management was not a requirement, and in times of emergency it broke down. The chancellor and his army of clerks and inspectors set and supervised the rules for barter, and collected their quota of tax in every form. The economy, self-sufficient in so many respects, worked on almost independently, driven by the engine of the NILE and the apparently unlimited natural resources of the country. *See also* TRADE.

Edfu

An ancient site in UPPER EGYPT, south of THEBES, on the western
bank of the NILE. Human habitation here has been dated far back
into the Palaeolithic age. In dynastic times it was famed as a centre of the cult of HORUS, its temple the home of the TRIAD of Horus,
Hathor and their child, Horus-Harakhte, the rising sun. At one time
it was thought to be the source of the Horus cult, before that was
traced back to the DELTA. The temple at Edfu was last reconstructed
by the Ptolemaic kings in the post-dynastic period, and it remains
exceptionally well preserved, with circuit wall, courtyard, HYPO-
STYLE HALL and sanctuary. The Greeks called Edfu Apollinopolis,
equating Horus with their own sun-god, Apollo.

education

Most Egyptians had no formal education. They were illiterate and
only basically numerate, as might be required by a particular trade.
They acquired their skills and knowledge through handed-down
wisdom and stories, example and observation, and personal expe-
rience. Among the wealthy, education in the intellectual sense
would be provided only for the sons (although the deity of writing
was a goddess, Seshat). The daughters would learn domestic skills
and graces, music and expressive dance, but not normally to read,
write or deal with numbers. In the OLD and MIDDLE KINGDOMS,
families normally employed tutors, trained scribes, to teach the
boys, and this remained the norm for the upper levels of society.
During the Middle Kingdom, schools were set up within the temples as part of the wide-ranging functions of these institutions.
The pupils would be the sons of members of the official class,
destined themselves to follow in their fathers' footsteps as clerks
of works, tax inspectors or land surveyors. Their lessons were taken

up with copying and re-copying classic texts, and chanting by rote, in a narrow curriculum that did not go beyond reading, writing and arithmetic. It was doubtless very tedious, and the trainee scribes were frequently beaten to encourage them, as well as being warned that if they failed to stay the course, manual labour, poverty and annual forced work on building sites awaited them. The methods of teaching explain the conventionality of much of Egyptian literary writing, the recurrence of identical phrases and word structures going straight back to the wearily assimilated thought patterns drubbed into the writers at school.

Egypt

The country occupying the NILE Valley, below the first cataract. Its extraordinary shape was dictated by the river: 750 miles (1,207 kilometres) long, but hardly more than 30 miles (48 kilometres) wide at its broadest, except on the Mediterranean coast, where the delta spread out to over 100 miles (161 kilometres). The Nile was both the country's reason for being and its defining feature. The word 'Egypt' is Greek, and in the *Iliad*, Homer takes it first to mean 'the great river' and secondarily the country, expressing the sense that the country was the gift of the river. The empty desert and scrub that stretched away for thousands of miles west and hundreds of miles east also helped in the formation of Egypt as a political unit, by creating a wide barrier between it and the states that arose simultaneously or later in the Near East and in Africa. The borders of ancient Egypt were never fully defined and shifted according to circumstances. The SINAI Peninsula, for example, was not at first regarded as Egypt but as an empty zone. In the imperial expansion of the NEW KINGDOM, the Egyptians boasted that their frontier was at the Euphrates, far off in Mesopotamia.

Egyptians

The NILE Valley has been inhabited by man and his ancestors for more than a million years. Remains found near the temples of ABU SIMBEL in NUBIA date far back into the Old Stone (Palaeolithic) Age, some 700,000 years. Around 25,000 years ago, climatic changes were bringing about the vast growth of the Sahara Desert, and peoples who had lived in that region moved eastwards, in the process becoming fishers as well as hunters. Around 6000 BC permanent signs of AGRICULTURE can be traced. In the PRE-DYNASTIC PERIOD, it was occupied by early peoples both from North Africa and East Africa, followed by Semitic nomads from Asia.

Egyptology

The scholarly study of ancient Egypt in all its aspects. For 1,700 years, the relics of ancient Egypt were disturbed only by tomb breakers in search of precious metals and by travellers, who admired or deplored but understood very little. In the 17th and 18th centuries, a number of European savants became interested in the fragmentary remains (still far more than we see today) and drew plans of certain sites. The English mathematician John Greaves published the first book devoted wholly to the PYRAMIDS in 1646. It was the French army's expedition to Egypt, under Napoleon Bonaparte, in 1799 that galvanized the process. Although it was part of a war campaign, a smaller ARMY of scholars, surveyors and scientists went with the main force, and the result of their work was the huge *Description de l'Egypte*. Masses of documents and artefacts were gathered and studied. By 1822, CHAMPOLLION had penetrated the secrets of HIEROGLYPHICS, and the ancient civilization began to reveal itself in detail. The result was an ever-growing demand for Egyptian artefacts from the many new museums established in western capitals. The process by which these items were acquired was little short of looting, although in theory it was officially controlled. Since the Napoleonic expedition, France has been in the vanguard of Egyptological studies, and Auguste MARIETTE was the first great fieldworker, although his methods were crude and arbitrary. However, he persuaded the authorities to set up the National Antiquities Service, with the aim of stopping the flood of antiquities out of the country and of setting up a properly managed national collection. Mariette's successors, Brugsch and MASPERO, and the British archaeologist Sir Flinders PETRIE laid the basis of modern Egyptology around the turn of the 19th century. Major discoveries were still to be made, including AMARNA (1914), the tomb of TUTANKHAMUN (1922), the great boat of CHEOPS (1954), and more will undoubtedly follow. Egyptologists of all nations campaigned to prevent the immersion of some of the greatest monuments of NUBIA when the ASWAN High Dam was built in the 1960s. Egyptology is still a young science, and its true purpose is not to unearth fabulous, heroic monuments of the past but to use every modern technique, including radiocarbon dating, aerial photography, computer analysis and projection, to establish the details of the beginnings, progressive stages and end of the great civilization. That beginning, with each new discovery, is pushed further and further into the remote past.

Eighteenth Dynasty

The first dynasty (1552–1314/1295 BC) of the NEW KINGDOM. The first king was AHMOSIS, who reigned 1552–1526 BC. Having driven the HYKSOS from Egypt, the king turned his attention southwards and set out to regain NUBIA from the local rulers. After three campaigns he succeeded, and then took his ARMY into Palestine, where he annexed the ports of the Phoenician coast, which were strategically placed for Egypt's timber imports. Ahmosis married his sister Nefertari, a popular queen whose cult was followed for some centuries after her death. Their son, AMENOPHIS I, succeeded in 1526 BC and continued the pushing outwards of Egypt's frontiers, and by the beginning of the following reign, it was stated that Egypt's border was the River Euphrates. Amenophis I was followed by TUTHMOSIS I (reigned 1506–1493 BC), son of a CONCUBINE, who reinforced his claim to the throne by marrying his half-sister. His son, Tuthmosis II, had to fight down revolts in the occupied lands. He died, leaving a six-year old son by a concubine and two daughters by his queen. The boy was TUTHMOSIS III, but the regency was assumed by his aunt, HATSHEPSUT (ruled 1478–1458 BC), wife and half-sister to Tuthmosis II. Hatshepsut proclaimed herself pharaoh and assumed the full honours of the position. During her rule, the focus of government was switched to internal administration, and the generals, who had gained a taste for campaigning abroad and accumulating rich tribute from the conquered tribesmen, became restive and hostile. On the death, or perhaps the deposition, of Hatshepsut, Tuthmosis III eventually acceded to the throne and became an extremely active military ruler, the greatest general among the kings of Egypt. His rule was spent almost entirely on campaign (17 in all) or on inspections of his growing empire. The record of his victories is found on the walls of KARNAK, which received much of the booty. Under Tuthmosis III the conquests of the Egyptians became more organized. He brought the sons of Syrian noblemen back to THEBES, both as hostages for their fathers' good behaviour and to be taught the lifestyle and manners of the Egyptian nobility. As the power of

Egypt spread farther, the opposition grew stronger. Tuthmosis III overcame numerous coalitions of enemy states and floated his army on rafts across the Euphrates to defeat the powerful MITANNI on their own territory. Egypt by this time was the greatest power in her own world (they were unaware of the existence of China). Tribute was received from Babylon, from Assyria, from the Hatti and Mitanni kingdoms, from Crete and other Mediterranean islands. Within Africa he pushed farther south than any pharaoh before him. No doubt remembering his own long frustration, he made his son, AMENOPHIS II, co-ruler in the year before his death. Amenophis II (ruled 1425–1401 BC) was a man of great physical stature and as warlike as his father, maintaining the empire with a ferocity untypical of the Egyptians as a whole. He was followed by Tuthmosis IV (ruled 1401–1390 BC), who, in a break with tradition, took as his wife a foreign princess, Mutemuya, daughter of the Mitannian king. By now, with empires confronting each other (the HITTITE power was growing rapidly in Anatolia), diplomacy was an essential part of statecraft and a diplomatic marriage was possible. Mutemuya was the mother of AMENOPHIS III (ruled 1390–1352 BC). Perhaps the incorporation of other traditions into the royal household accounts for his style of kingship. Unlike his energetic predecessors, he pursued a life of luxury and leisure in the most opulent court that Egypt had ever known. He married a commoner, TIY, who was given the new title of Great Royal Wife, although he also maintained a vast harem. In the course of this reign there is no doubt that Asiatic influences were strong, not only on dress and culture but also on religion, which remained at the heart of Egyptian life and thought. In the regions around, there was a growing emphasis on the worship of the sun as supreme, or even sole, deity. It was at this time that the cult of ATEN, rather than that of AMUN, began to grow, especially in court circles. But the priesthood of Amun-Ra at THEBES, whose wealth and power had grown with the absences of the warrior pharaohs and the indolence of Amenophis III, remained strong and jealous of its prestige and power. The Aten was championed by HELIOPOLIS, whose ancient predominance had long since been overtaken by Thebes.

With the reign of Amenophis IV (ruled 1352–1338 BC) the royal break to Aten was made complete. The king changed his name to AKHENATEN and moved the capital from Thebes to a new site, el-AMARNA, where he had a city built that he called Akhetaten, with a vast temple to Aten at its centre. Akhenaten's obsession with religion led him to ignore the fact that the empire was under serious threat. The Hittite king, Suppiliulumas, was forging alliances among the kingdoms and princedoms that paid tribute to Egypt. The prince of Kadesh invaded Syria, the Phoenician coast was lost to Amurru, and the Palestinians captured the fortresses of Megiddo and Jerusalem. The losses are chronicled in the Amarna Letters, stored carefully at Akhetaten and apparently ignored by the king. Akhenaten and his queen, NEFERTITI, had no son, although several daughters. His two immediate successors were legitimized by marrying royal daughters. The second of these was Tutankhaten. His name was altered to TUTANKHAMUN by the priests of AMUN-RA at Thebes, who busied themselves in rooting out the worship of the Aten and restoring the tradition. Tutankhamun's fame is wholly due to the fact that his tomb, uniquely among the pharaohs, was discovered intact in the 20th century. He was an ineffectual and short-lived ruler. Authority lay with the priesthood and with the army leader, HOREMHEB, who had regained much of the territory lost in Asia. After Tutankhamun's early death, Horemheb assumed the throne (ruled c.1323–1295 BC). A member of the provincial nobility, he was an austere figure who dated his reign from the death of Amenophis III, as though the AMARNA PERIOD had never been. He held the frontier at the Lebanon and restored internal order. He may have married a princess of the Tuthmosid house to establish legitimacy as a ruler, but he left no son and, by pre-arrangement, on his death the kingship passed to another general, RAMESES I, the first king of the NINETEENTH DYNASTY.

Eighth Dynasty

A dynasty (c.2200–2160 BC) of the FIRST INTERMEDIATE PERIOD. The kings were based at MEMPHIS and ruled only the area around Memphis. The DELTA area was occupied by invaders (described as 'Asiatics' by the Egyptians) who had come across SINAI. THEBES and HERAKLEOPOLIS were rival states to Memphis. All were determined to restore the unity of Egypt and to resurrect the grandeurs of the OLD KINGDOM, but first they had one another to contend with. The Memphite kings claimed that theirs was the legitimate rule, but the other rulers were equally ready to proclaim their pedigrees. It was a confused and ill-recorded period with many brief reigns and no outstanding figures.

Elephantine

A site on the southern tip of Elephantine Island, in the NILE a little way above the first cataract, a NOME capital (of the Elephant nome), its history going back to the early period of the OLD KINGDOM. The original brick shrine was covered by a succession of later temples, with much destruction of the preceding work, but even in the final EIGHTEENTH DYNASTY structure, the sanctuary is still linked to the original sanctuary through several successive levels and epochs of building. Many charms and votive objects have been recovered from the site.

Eleventh Dynasty

First dynasty of the MIDDLE KINGDOM. Known as the Theban Dynasty (2040–1991 BC), it was founded by Inyotef I who gained control of UPPER EGYPT from HERAKLEOPOLIS. His successors contested MIDDLE EGYPT with KHETI III of the TENTH DYNASTY, extending their dominion upriver into NUBIA. The Eleventh Dynasty made steady gains until the final victory under MENTUHOTPE II, who defeated Herakleopolis to become undisputed king of Upper and LOWER EGYPT (ruled 2040–2009 BC). This dynasty marks the end of the FIRST INTERMEDIATE PERIOD and the start of the Middle Kingdom, which would last a further 1,500 years. At first there was pacification to be done, and the power of the NOMARCHS, already broken in Lower Egypt by the TENTH DYNASTY, had to be reduced in Upper Egypt also. They ceased to be hereditary, except those of BENI-HASAN, who had been allies of the Thebans. Mentuhotpe II revived the system of centralized administration but without the stifling absolutism of the OLD KINGDOM. The law considered all men to be equal, and the kings of the Middle Kingdom spent much time and thought on the administration of justice. With a return to regular floodings of the NILE, prosperity had already begun to climb, and the stability introduced under the Middle Kingdom accelerated the growth. At this time the cult of AMUN-RA, who had been the war-god of the Thebans in their victorious campaign, took its full form, encouraged by the monarchy and provided with a powerful priesthood and immensely rich endowments. With the death of Mentuhotpe IV· around 1991 BC, the dynasty comes to a rather sudden and obscure end for a line that had accomplished so much.

Eloquent Peasant

An episode recorded in literature from the early MIDDLE KING-

DOM, attesting the sense of humour of the Pharaoh Achthoes II. A peasant who had grounds for complaint against a greedy steward argued his case so forcefully and vividly, first before the VIZIER, finally before the pharaoh, that he had to restate it nine times. The tale makes a contrast with the far more ample evidence of procedural formality and heavy convention when the pharaoh met his people in the flesh.

ennead

A group of nine deities. The most famous ennead was the Heliopolitan, comprising RA-ATUM, SHU, Tefnut, GEB, NUT, OSIRIS, ISIS, NEPHTHYS and SETH. *See also* COSMOLOGY.

eroticism

The ancient Egyptians were no different from the rest of humanity in their interest in the erotic aspects of life. Throughout the dynasties there is evidence of intense interest. Pornographic pictures and writings were inscribed on valuable papyri. Love charms were universally believed in, and recipes for aphrodisiacs abounded. THEBES, MEMPHIS and no doubt other places of pilgrimage, had thriving brothels. The squat fertility god, MIN, whose cult centre was at KOPTOS, presided cheerfully over all this activity, but most major gods had some connection with the cult of fertility.

Esarhaddon

King of Assyria and conqueror of Egypt in 671 BC, defeating Pharaoh Taharqa of the Nubian Dynasty. He proclaimed, 'I laid siege to MEMPHIS, his royal residence, and captured it in half a day by means of mines, breaches and assault ladders. His queen, the women of his palace, his heir apparent, his other children,

his possessions, horses, large and small, cattle beyond counting
I carried away as plunder to Assyria.'

execration texts

These texts, often found on magical figurines in the ELEVENTH
and TWELFTH DYNASTIES, list foreign enemy peoples whom the
rulers of Egypt wished to see dead. As was usually the case in
such lists, they include both long-vanquished enemies as well
as contemporary threats.

exodus

The Biblical exodus of the Jews may have occurred in the reign
of RAMESES II, although no Egyptian written source refers to
these events. There is archaeological evidence of an immigrant
people, known as the APIRU, quarry workers and brick-makers,
who may have been the Hebrew people.

Eye of Horus

In his epic battle with SETH, HORUS lost an eye, which was later
reassembled by THOTH. This was the eye painted on the prow of
Egyptian ships and much used as a protective AMULET. It is also
found use as a measure for grain—perhaps as a precaution
against unfair dealing. It was divided into six portions—a half,
a quarter, an eighth, a sixteenth, a thirty-second, and a sixty-
fourth. A full barrel (approximately $8^{1}/_{2}$ pints/4 litres) was equivalent to a full Eye.

F

faience
Decorative pottery, made from a quartz paste with a glazed surface, sometimes inlaid with GOLD or other precious metals, used for dishes, jars, medallions, tiles, etc.

Faiyum
A fertile area to the west of the NILE Valley, south of the DELTA, which was empty marshland during the OLD KINGDOM but was drained and exploited in the MIDDLE KINGDOM.

false door *see* STELE.

famine
A series of low INUNDATIONS, around the end of the SIXTH DYNASTY, coincided with political unrest and led to famine in UPPER EGYPT, with a contemporary record claiming that parents ate their own children and many other texts attesting to the hardship suffered by the people. The weakness of central government at this time exacerbated the problems caused by a temporary but drastic climatic change.

female kings *see* HATSHEPSUT, NITOCRIS, SOBEKNEFERU, TWOSRE.

festival
The Egyptian year was liberally punctuated by the festivals of

gods and by other events, such as a king's jubilee (SED FESTIVAL), or a crown prince's wedding. The Sed Festival in theory celebrated 30 years, but an elderly man becoming king might hold his after a much shorter period of ruling. Particularly at important religious centres like ABYDOS, festivals came in almost constant succession and demanded careful administration. At MEDINET HABU in the time of Rameses III there were 60 festivals in the year, and a CALENDAR of feasts and offerings was kept in order to record what provision should be made for each. The feasting aspect was taken literally, and a major festival like the feast of the god Seker required 3,694 loaves, 410 cakes, and 905 jars of BEER for the celebrants.

Processions were a feature of festivals. The image of the god, escorted by other gods and by images of bygone kings, was brought forth on a boat-shaped vehicle (*see* SHIPS AND SHIPBUILDING) and taken on a ceremonial route, with regular stopping places, watched by huge crowds.

Fifteenth, Sixteenth and Seventeenth Dynasties

These span the SECOND INTERMEDIATE PERIOD (*c.*1674–1553 BC). The first king was Salitis (the dates of individual reigns at this time are unclear). He appears to have had total control of Lower and MIDDLE EGYPT, and the HYKSOS contacts extended to NUBIA, which had regained independence. Salitis and his successors took over the administrative and religious machine of Egypt and let it work for them with very little in the way of change. They assumed the pharaonic role. Based first of all at AVARIS in the DELTA, where they set up a SETH cult that identified Seth also with the foreign gods Baal and Teshub, the capital moved to MEMPHIS. The third Hyksos king, Apophis I, ceded some of his power to a branch of the family that was classed as the Sixteenth Dynasty in MANETHO's list. The Hyksos dynasty took its pharaonic responsibilities seriously and encouraged building, the arts and crafts, and literature, although the upsurge of national feeling in the NEW KINGDOM was to brand them as despoilers. The famous mathematical PAPYRUS, known as the Rhind Papyrus, now in the British Museum, dates from Apophis I. It was a time of considerable technical innovation. The Hyksos brought Egypt the horse harness and the war chariot, and their military improvements were in due course to assist the later growth of the empire. In the south, some time after 1650 BC, an Egyptian dynasty emerged at THEBES, tracing its origins back to the THIRTEENTH Dynasty; its founder was Rahotep. With the apparent tolerance of the Hyksos (there may have been marriage links), they ruled UPPER EGYPT, in poorer circumstances than the northern kings, building themselves PYRAMIDS of mud brick. Eventually strife broke out between the two dynasties, under the Theban kings, Ta'a and his successors, Seqenenre (whose mummy shows evidence of a violent death) and Kamose. The Hyksos were being forced back on the Delta. Kamose, too, may have died in battle, but his successor, AHMOSIS, completed the task and drove the Hyksos out of Egypt, becoming the founder of the mighty EIGHTEENTH Dynasty, the first in the NEW KINGDOM.

Fifth Dynasty

A dynasty (2510–2460 BC) of the OLD KINGDOM, which had strong hereditary links with the preceding one. The first king, Userkaf ('powerful is his KA') also retained officials from the previous reign. The Fifth-Dynasty kings traced their origins back to HELIOPOLIS and therefore were keen adherents of the sun-god cult. Userkaf built a SUN TEMPLE at ABUSIR. During his reign there were

Fifth Dynasty

Egypt's first recorded contacts with the ancient Greek kingdoms, with luxury items including jars and furniture being exported. The Fifth Dynasty saw a growth in contact with the countries beyond Egypt to the north, east and south, including the first recorded expeditions to the tropical land of PUNT. Userkaf's successor, Sahure, employed warships on the Mediterranean coast, although contacts on the whole were peaceful. The power and splendour of the pharaohs were becoming known to their neighbours, and Egypt was perceived as a source not only of marvellously made things but also of magic power and arcane knowledge. Relations were on a trading level rather than diplomatic— the era of empires had not yet come. Little is known about the kings Neferirkare-Kakai and Shepsesre, but Nefererfre's MORTUARY TEMPLE, found with a great stock of papyri, inscribed plaques, model boats, carved figures of prisoners, and sculptures of the king himself, is an important source of knowledge on the period. It was during the later reigns of the Fifth Dynasty, with Pharaohs Neuserre, Isesi (Djedkare) and WENIS, that the iron hand of central control began gradually to slip. These kings are most closely identified with the sun cult, which rose to a peak unequalled until the EIGHTEENTH DYNASTY. As the personage of the monarch became ever-more codified as divine, so the power of the provincial governors and the senior officials of the court became greater and more independent. Instead of being grouped in annexes to the king's tomb, important functionaries constructed their own mounuments, as seen in the great MASTABA of Ti at Saqqara. He was Chief Barber to the Royal Household and Controller of Lakes and Farmland. The peasantry remained heavily oppressed, depersonalized by the arbitrary conscription of the labour battalions, obliged to labour both for the king and the

NOMARCH, and victims both of fighting between the rival power centres and of shortages caused by lack of administration.

First and Second Dynasties

During the five centuries of these two lines of kings, also known as the THINITE PERIOD, from the name of the city of This to which the first kings traced their origin, and lasting from 3150 to 2700 BC, ancient Egyptian society developed the basic form that was to continue throughout. The first king, AHA, is credited with achievements that may have both preceded and followed him, although he was certainly a strong ruler who set the pattern for the intensive control of land and people that was characteristic of the early dynasties of the OLD KINGDOM. There was warfare with LIBYA and NUBIA during his reign. He worked hard to promote the new-found unity of the two kingdoms, and had tombs at SAQQARA, close to MEMPHIS, at the southern extreme of LOWER EGYPT, and at ABYDOS in UPPER EGYPT. The next recorded king is Djer, who continued to make war in NUBIA and Libya and otherwise maintained the policies set in motion by Aha. His principal residence was at Memphis, but his tomb was at Abydos. This king, whose tomb, surrounded by those of his courtiers, was clearly one of great wealth, may have been the source of the legend of OSIRIS's earthly reign. Osiris's heart was said to be buried at ABYDOS, and Djer's campaigns through Egypt and into Nubia can be compared to the scattering of Osiris's fragments through the country. The high point of the First Dynasty was reached with the lengthy reign of DEN, another energetic king whose attention seems to have been directed more across SINAI in the direction of Asia. Den, too, worked to placate Lower Egypt and establish full union. His rule may have lasted for as long as

First and Second Dynasties

fifty years, and his is the first SED FESTIVAL of which we have a record. He is the first king to add the third name to his set of titles: the *nsw-bty*, or 'king of Upper and Lower Egypt name'. In his case it was Khasty, meaning 'man of the desert', a reference to his military excursions. His successor, Anedjib, initiated a further development of the pharaonic title, with the 'two lords' name', the name placed under the protection of both HORUS and SETH and so reconciling the dualism of the gods of north and south, field and desert, in the person of the king. It also underlines the king's possession of the destructive powers of SETH. The last king of the First Dynasty was Ka'a. The reasons for the change of dynasty are obscure, although Ka'a's predecessor, Semerkhet, may have been considered illegitimate. In a practice that was often to be repeated by kings of dubious claim, he erased Anedjib's name from the commemorative vases produced for that king's *Sed* Festival.

The Second Dynasty located itself firmly at Memphis and built up strong contacts with the DELTA region. During this succession of kings, the cult of the sun-god RA gradually became established. Upper Egypt may have been neglected or developed a separatist tendency as a result of the fondness of the kings for northern deities like BASTET, the Delta CAT-goddess, and a separate line of priest-kings developed at ABYDOS. This political divide came to an end with the firm rule of Khasekhem, whose Horus name means 'the powerful one is crowned', later changed to Khesekemwy, 'the two powers are crowned'. His origins were from HERAKLEOPOLIS in Upper Egypt, and he imposed his rule on the north. This reign marks the beginning of substantial stone ARCHITECTURE, including his own tomb at Abydos, and opens the way to the achievements of the THIRD DYNASTY.

First Intermediate Period

(2200–2040 BC) The somewhat undescriptive title is used to cover the transitional age between the OLD and the NEW KINGDOMS. As its vagueness suggests, there is not complete agreement among Egyptologists about the beginning or the duration of this period, taken by some to begin with the SEVENTH DYNASTY and by others with the NINTH DYNASTY. As the Seventh and EIGHTH Dynasties together only occupied a span of some 20 years and presided over a state of growing confusion, there is good reason to take the Seventh Dynasty as the start of the First Intermediate Period, which continues for around 150 years and is characterized by a continuous internal struggle for power that went on until the accession of MENTUHOTPE II around 2040 BC. This struggle is essentially the rivalry between HERAKLEOPOLIS and THEBES. The Eighth Dynasty, centred at MEMPHIS, soon succumbed to the warlike rulers of Herakleopolis who supplied the Ninth and TENTH Dynasties, whose area of control fluctuated from LOWER and MIDDLE EGYPT to almost the whole country. The Theban claimants established the ELEVENTH DYNASTY at about the same time, and the two were locked in combat until the fifth Theban king, Mentuhotpe II, defeated Herakleopolis and finally established the Theban kingship over the two lands.

The anguish and introspection forced on the Egyptians during the turbulent era of the First Intermediate Period are revealed in the writings of the time, which are sombre and pessimistic in tone. The age-old system had broken down. The individual Egyptian felt a greater responsibility for himself, and this altered his perception of the AFTERLIFE too. Everyone would now face the court of Osiris and defend his own record on earth, not in terms of good or bad but in terms of having upheld or disturbed the proper balance

flint

of life. This spiritual development paralleled the gradual improvements in the life of the peasantry, brought about the resumption of 'normal' floods, and by a less arbitrary and impersonal social policy following the revolts of the late OLD KINGDOM.

flint

Deposits of flints are found widely in Egypt and were extensively worked during the dynastic era. Even late on, flint-bladed implements were used by the poorer peasants and craftsmen.

Fourteenth Dynasty *see* THIRTEENTH AND FOURTEENTH DYNASTIES.

Fourth Dynasty

The second dynasty of the OLD KINGDOM (2625–2510 BC). Its first king was SNOFRU who ruled 2625–2600 BC, or perhaps longer. He led an expedition into NUBIA to crush a revolt there, and also fought the Libyans, and extended Egyptian dominion into the SINAI PENINSULA. These campaigns all had an economic motivation, to secure access to valuable mineral reserves and quarries, and to protect trade routes. Snofru is credited with taking huge numbers of prisoners and cattle on his southern and eastern campaigns, whilst the Sinai expedition enabled Egypt to exploit the COPPER, malachite and turquoise of the region. Snofru was a shipbuilder and sent ships to Lebanon for timber; he was also a great builder in stone. Three PYRAMIDS are ascribed to him, the first at MAIDUM, near Saqqara, modelled on the step pyramid constructed by IMHOTEP for Djoser. He then built two more pyramids farther north, at DAHSHUR. Snofru was succeeded by CHEOPS, whose name is linked to his own monument, the Great Pyramid, although his remains were robbed from it some time in antiquity. The actual details of Cheops's reign are not well known. By this time the central power of the kings was fully established and exercised in an absolute way. The desire to build ever greater funerary monuments drove the organization of the state to an extreme of management, which dehumanized the bulk of the population and created the complex bureaucracy that overlooked every aspect of life. After Cheops the succession went first to his son, Djedefre, and then to Djedefre's half-brother, CHEPHREN. Chephren commissioned the sculpting of the Great SPHINX. He took a strong interest in theology and during his reign the combined diety RA-ATUM was fully developed. His son, MYCERINUS, is the occupant of the third and smallest pyramid of the GIZA complex. Shepseskaf, last king of the Fourth Dynasty, took as his queen Khentkawes, who was descended from Djedefre's other half-brother, Djedefhor, in what seems to have been a deliberate attempt to unify the strands of the royal family. He broke from the pyramid tradition for his own tomb, having it built in the form of a giant SARCOPHAGUS in the southern part of SAQQARA.

funerary practice

The essence of Egyptian funerary practice at all times was to provide the best set of circumstances to perpetuate the dead person in the AFTERLIFE. Almost, if not entirely, alone among ancient peoples, they believed that the physical body was necessary after DEATH. The origins of this belief are unfathomable, although in PRE-DYNASTIC times, when burial was a matter of wrapping the corpse in an animal's hide and burying it, with accessories, in a pit in the sand, the corpse was often well preserved by the arid soil. Later, the preservation was assisted by the dismemberment of the corpse, which was placed in its grave in a tidy package of bony parts, with the skull set on top. With greater social cohesion, greater wealth and the tendency of all processes to become more elaborate in such circumstances, the funeral arrangements became more substantial. The MASTABA began to appear, in a simple form, as a monument above the grave, and a framework of mythology also arose, to provide explanation, reason and justification for the whole business (*see also* COSMOLOGY, OSIRIS, UNDERWORLD).

Alongside the accretion of myth directly related to death and the afterlife grew the concept of the god-king. In the OLD KINGDOM view, only the king achieved heaven, and the funeral of a god had to be of divine grandeur, so that when he joined RA in the sky, he would have sufficient retinue and provisions to be accepted as worthy. Such a view might have implied a hecatomb, with the death or suicide of wives and courtiers. This did not happen in Egypt, where respect for the life force was deeply ingrained. Instead, the king departed with a multitude of little figures whom the magic of religion would turn into servants and attendants. He was provided with furnishings, clothes, tools, weapons—everything that he used in life he would use again in death. Thus the ever larger tomb was filled with ever more objects. The STELE, or false door, that had originally carried only the king's name bore a list of all the offerings that should be presented to maintain the king suitably. Since the body, however well preserved, might decay eventually, effigies of the king were placed in the tomb, marked with his unique name in its CARTOUCHE. By the THIRD DYNASTY, the mastaba had evolved into the funerary complex of the PYRAMID, with satellite constructions functioning as MORTUARY TEMPLES, processional courts, store rooms, symbolic cenotaphs, tombs of courtiers and relatives, and dwellings for priest-attendants and guards. The point of entrance was the valley temple: this was equivalent to the quay at which the dead king embarked on a voyage, the final destination of which was the sky, although it was a place of reception rather than of departure. Every step from here to the tomb chamber was provided with a symbolic value. The valley temple itself was under the protection of the lion-goddess SEKHMET. In the tomb of the FIFTH-DYNASTY king, Neuserre, she is shown suckling him. A processional causeway led up to the MORTUARY TEMPLE; that of WENIS at SAQQARA is 700 metres (2,296 feet) long, roofed and decorated with scenes of life on the royal domains, scenes of the building of the temple itself and auspicious episodes of the king's life. The mortuary temple was placed at the north face of early pyramids, but from the FOURTH DYNASTY was set on the eastern face, towards the rising sun. This temple had a vestibule leading to a courtyard, with a sanctum beyond. Statues of the king and of his family were placed in the temple to receive offerings. The statues themselves were the object of considerable attention (*see* PHARAOH'S DAY). Hunting and warfare were the primary motifs of the mortuary temple's decoration. Close to the pyramid were the BOAT PITS, in which lay the wooden barques in which the king could travel with RA. The SARCOPHAGUS of the king was solemnly borne into the pyramid itself. The entrance was in the north face and led down to a vestibule, past three protective granite portcullises to an antechamber. On the east side was the SERDAB, where statues of the king were placed. On the west side was the tomb chamber. This relatively simple design lasted until the TWELFTH DYNASTY. The corridors of the last Fifth-Dynasty king, WENIS, and subsequent kings, were decorated with the PYRAMID TEXTS. These esoteric spells and charms, hidden within the pyramid, written by privileged scribes, preserved the ritual that would safely see the dead king past all obstacles and achieve his ascension to the sky, his assimilation with Ra and Osiris.

The coffin also evolved in use and significance. The Fourth Dynasty coffin appeared to represent a house for the deceased, decorated to resemble a palace facade and rectangular in shape, in effect another 'false door' through which the KA could pass. From the SIXTH DYNASTY it was inscribed with texts and its function became more clearly similar to that of the boat that conveyed the dead man through the dangerous region between life and death. From MIDDLE KINGDOM times, the shape of the coffin gradually became rounded and approximated the outline of the body. The coffin was also enclosed in the much larger and more substantial sarcophagus, made of stone or carved from the living rock. At the close of the funeral ceremony, the door to the coffin chamber was closed and sealed. It was intended never to be reopened.

By Middle Kingdom times, the view of the afterlife had changed. It was no longer the prerogative of the king and his HONOURED ONES. Tombs were erected by many others, equally anxious to provide for their long future. The tomb of a high functionary was a compressed version of his royal master's: a vestibule decorated with pictures of the properties of the dead man, a courtyard decorated with scenes of everyday life and of the preparation of the tomb. Store rooms are decorated with scenes of BAKING and brewing. The chapel would include family scenes, pictures of harvest and SACRIFICE, each with its allotted position in the overall design (*see* ART). In the Middle Kingdom, a tomb would also include finely detailed and painted models of the animals, slaves, boats and farm buildings belonging to or administered by the tomb's occupant.

The formalities of a funeral, as shown in the typical decorative scheme, include mourning the dead, with weeping mourners gathered around the corpse, then accompanying it to the house of embalmment. The next stages had to await the process of MUMMIFICATION. Then the body was brought to the NECROPOLIS, where its tomb had been prepared. Within the confines, ritual visits were enacted, to SAIS and to BUTO, with offerings made. Then the final offerings were made, and purifications performed with incense. A symbolic drama accompanied the drawing of the coffin into the tomb, with one priest striving to pull the coffin back towards life while another pulled it towards its tomb. This procedure was watched over by the *tekenu*, a human form wrapped in an animal skin, a protective spirit of the necropolis, as the coffin was drawn into the tomb, at whose entrance the funeral feast was laid out. The articles to serve the spirit of the dead were placed in position, and finally the coffin went in, with a statue of the deceased, representing him as a pilgrim to ABYDOS, burial place of OSIRIS. The rites of protection were enunciated, and then the chamber was sealed.

G

games

The Egyptians enjoyed board and table games, and there is evidence of a variety of games from PRE-DYNASTIC times onwards. The oldest gaming board in the world was found in a Pre-dynastic cemetery at El-Mahasna, eight miles (13 kilometres) north of ABYDOS; it is made of clay. Actual games, like *han* (the jar game), can be traced back to the FIFTH DYNASTY. Games were among the diversions of the AFTERLIFE as well as daily life, and the tomb of TUTANKHAMUN yielded game boards, with lots and knucklebones to cast. Numerous temples have game boards carved or scratched in their stonework, clearly done for the entertainment of the workmen.

Geb

The earth-god in the Heliopolitan COSMOLOGY, from whose union with the sky-goddess, NUT, came the four children ISIS, OSIRIS, SETH and Nephthys. It is Geb who presides at the court of the gods that assigns the kingship of Egypt to HORUS rather than to Seth.

Gebel Barkal

Temple site in NUBIA, close to NAPATA. The temple had been dedicated to AMUN by TUTHMOSIS III, and it was greatly enlarged by the Nubian king PIANKHY (TWENTY-FIFTH DYNASTY), who mod-

elled it on KARNAK, with a HYPOSTYLE HALL, fronted by a pylon, a
PERISTYLE COURT fronted by another pylon, and an avenue of
CRIOSPHINXES (these he removed from a temple of AMENOPHIS III
at Soleb).

Gerza

This site in UPPER EGYPT, important in PRE-DYNASTIC times, has
given its name to a phase of Pre-dynastic culture, also known as
Naqada, after another Upper Egypt site.

Gerzean Period *see* PRE-DYNASTIC PERIOD.

Giza

The site of the most spectacular PYRAMID complex, including the
Great Pyramid, the Great SPHINX and many other monuments in
a vast funerary complex spanning the range of dynastic history.
Set on a plateau a few miles southwest of modern Cairo, it was
originally selected because it had good stone for QUARRYING. The
quarry faces themselves were then used for rock-cut tombs. The
site was developed from early in the OLD KINGDOM.

gods

There are more than 2,000 gods who were worshipped at some
time or another, and in some place or another, by the ancient
Egyptians. This vast array is further complicated by changings
and mergings of identity. Gods originally were associated with
specific areas and retained this association until the collapse of
the whole Egyptian religious system. Each NOME had its protective god, from the PRE-DYNASTIC PERIOD on, and it was worshipped in the provincial capital. Sometimes it took on some of
the attributes of a greater god, especially those of RA, the sun-
god. All the gods were seen as having characteristics similar to

gold

those of people. They were subject to vanity, lechery, greed and drunkenness. Nor were they all-powerful; a strong man equipped with magic powers could influence the gods' behaviour. The gods were a higher manifestation of the same all-pervading life force that lived in man, bull and beetle, and in the richness of their own natures they could readily change or even share shapes. The Egyptians, who saw egg turn to tadpole and then to frog, saw nothing odd in a divinity being even more protean. They had a scanty knowledge of iron, derived mostly from the discovery of meteoritic fragments, and this may have been the cause of a supposition that the gods had bodies of iron. *See also* COSMOLOGY, RELIGION, THEOLOGY, INDIVIDUAL GOD NAMES.

gold

Gold was mined in parts of NUBIA and in the Eastern Desert, between the NILE Valley and the Red Sea. It was hammered and picked out of the veins in the rock. It was one of the most gruelling tasks in the Egyptian climate, and the labourers must often have been prisoners of war or criminals. Panning in that arid region, of course, was impossible. Gold was also obtained by military victory, and was the favourite form of tribute to be received by the conquering state from the defeated one. Egypt's gold became a matter of dreams and envy to neighbouring kingdoms. King Tushratta of MITANNI sent a message to the Egyptian king, saying 'In your land, my brother, gold is as common as dust'. *See also* JEWELLERY, METALWORK.

Golden Horus Name

One of the five names making up the royal title, from the TWELFTH DYNASTY onwards. It characterized the king's personal qualities, as with RAMESES II, 'rich in years, great in victories'.

granary

Egypt lived largely on the corn products of bread and BEER, and the annual grain crop had to be stored and made to last until the next harvest. OLD KINGDOM sources refer to two granaries, the Red Granary of LOWER EGYPT and the White Granary of UPPER EGYPT, just as they do to the two treasuries, also in the same symbolic colours. As the country expanded southwards down the NILE and the population grew in Lower Egypt, these two great granaries must have been complemented by other subsidiary storage points. Their prime importance may have been to hold the buffer stocks—the reserves that could be used in time of shortage, and whose value in the commercial life of Egypt was as great as the GOLD reserves of a modern state.

Great Ennead

The nine gods—RA and the eight deities whom he formed: SHU, Tefnut, GEB, NUT, SETH, NEPHTHYS, OSIRIS and ISIS. *See also* COSMOLOGY.

Great Pyramid *see* PYRAMID.

Great Sphinx *see* SPHINX.

greywacke

Extensively quarried at Wadi Hammamet, this hard grey-green stone, which can be polished to a fine sheen, was very widely used in building and also in sculpture, including some of the finest figure sculpture of the OLD KINGDOM period.

H

Haapi
God of the River NILE. He was believed to live above the first cataract and to be hermaphrodite.

Harakhte
A title of HORUS, identifying him with RA as god of the morning sun. The sun and moon were known as 'the two eyes of Horus'.

Hathor
A major goddess, the Lady of Heaven, Earth and the UNDERWORLD, worshipped throughout Egypt and indeed beyond as far as Syria. Portrayed as a cow or as a woman with the horned head of a cow, she was perceived as a helpful and gentle deity, with women especially under her protection in pregnancy and CHILDBIRTH. Most other goddesses in the pantheon laid claim to some attributes of Hathor, but she was supreme, as her relationship with HORUS indicates. She was his wet-nurse and later his wife. Her cult was centred at DENDERA in UPPER EGYPT, although there were temples to her throughout the country.

Hatshepsut
A female king of the EIGHTEENTH DYNASTY (ruled 1478–1458 BC). Daughter of the Pharaoh Thutmosis I and of the widow of AMENOPHIS I, she married her half-brother who became king as Tuthmosis II. They had no son, but a daughter, Neferure. In 1478 BC her husband

died, and Hatshepsut became regent to the six-year-old TUTHMOSIS III, a son of her husband by one of his concubines. After a short time she abandoned the regency and had herself proclaimed a king, with the names Maatkare Khnemet-Amun-Hatshepsut (MAAT is the *kha* of RA, 'she who embraces AMUN, foremost among women). As part of her claim to the throne, she associated her dead father with her rule and proclaimed herself the daughter of AMUN-RA. Hatshepsut was a competent ruler with no taste for warfare. The principal expedition of her reign was a peaceful commercial one to the land of PUNT. She reigned until 1458 BC, when TUTHMOSIS III at last regained the throne. There was no precedent for a queen regnant and Hatshepsut reigned as a female king, portrayed in some reliefs in male garments and without breasts. She was aided by a number of courtiers of relatively lowly origin who owed their position to her favour. After her death, the frustrated Tuthmosis III had her CARTOUCHE erased from her monuments.

Heh and Hehet *see* COSMOLOGY.

Heliopolis
Now a suburb of Cairo, but once a great centre of Egyptian religion, seat of the cult of the sun-god RA and the centre of the most widely accepted COSMOLOGY. The doctrine of Heliopolis spelled out how creation originally occurred, and the BEN-BEN stone fetish in the temple was a symbol of that creation.

henu *see* MEASUREMENT.

Herakleopolis
A settlement and NOME capital situated to the south of the FAIYUM region on a strategic north-south route. It was the home ground of the Herakleopolitan kings of the NINTH AND TENTH DYNASTIES,

who rose from being NOMARCHS to kings who at times controlled the whole country, at times only parts of Middle and Lower Egypt.

Herihor

A high priest (first prophet) of AMUN, in the reign of Rameses XI. In effect, during this period of enfeebled monarchy, he was the ruler of UPPER EGYPT, and his decorations on the walls of the Temple of KHONSU at KARNAK indicate the growth of his status and authority. He inaugurated the line of independent 'priest-kings' at THEBES that was to last for almost 200 years, in parallel to the TWENTY-FIRST and TWENTY-SECOND Dynasties.

Hermopolis Magna

(Latin and Greek: 'great city of Hermes', so called to distinguish it from the DELTA town of the same name) a temple city 187 miles (300 kilometres) south of Cairo and source of the Hermopolitan COSMOLOGY. Here the god SHU was said to have raised the sky above the earth. There are architectural remains here from many dynasties, including the last native Egyptian one.

Herodotus

A Greek traveller and historian who visited Egypt and recorded his impressions during the second half of the 5th century BC.

Hierakonpolis

An ancient site in UPPER EGYPT, about 62 miles (100 kilometres) south of THEBES. Tomb finds here go back to the GERZA period, 400–3300 BC. It was here that two COPPER statues were discovered, of the OLD KINGDOM Pharaoh PEPY I and his heir, Merenra.

hieratic

A form of writing that was developed from HIEROGLYPHICS. Hieratic (from Greek *Hieroatiks*, 'priestly') was devised in order to have a faster means of writing for non-sacred documents. Later, by the time of NEW KINGDOM, hieratic script was also used for sacred texts. *See also* HIEROGLYPHICS, DEMOTIC, WRITING.

hieroglyphics

(From the Greek words *hieros*, 'sacred', and *glyphos*, 'sculptured') the word was coined by the Greeks to describe the Egyptian inscriptions. Hieroglyphic WRITING was practised in Egypt for over 3,500 years, from before the FIRST DYNASTY until after the time of Christ. From the evidence available, it seems clear that this form of writing was devised in Egypt and not imported, although other ancient civilizations also developed script at the same time or slightly earlier. In its earliest form, it was a useful means of identifying ownership by means of a recognizable and repeatable symbol. In such a primitive form, this can hardly be considered writing, if writing is taken to be a means of expressing LANGUAGE. But the Egyptians demonstrated their understanding of the linkage of writing to speech by setting down, in front of the little drawing, an alphabetic sign to denote its actual sound. The earliest known hieroglyphs are found as seals, or seal impressions, and as identifying marks on vases, clay tablets and wooden boards. The basic concept of hieroglyphic writing is to provide a picture of the object the writer is describing. This has its limitations as soon as more complex or abstract concepts are introduced. The simple pictogram, or visual sign, was soon reinforced by the phonogram, a mark intended to represent a particular sound, and by the ideogram, which is a picture that represents something other than the apparent image, e.g. to demonstrate anger the Egyptians used the stylized picture of a baboon, a creature notorious for its bad temper. A further development of this was the determinative symbol, used to avoid confusion between words that shared a common image. In hieroglyphics, a word could be a simple pictogram or a combination of ideogram, phonogram and determinative symbol. This process was complete by the beginning of the dynastic era, providing a splendid tool for the compilation of lists, always a necessity as a monarchy became centralized and sought to exert a bureaucratic control over land and people.

Hieroglyphic writing is an ART form in itself, and it is of interest here that in early Egyptian the term for 'to write' and 'to draw' was the same. There are a host of different images, many of them giving an insight into the social life, and the plants, animals and birds of the OLD KINGDOM period. Even when other forms of writing, HIERATIC and DEMOTIC, replaced it for more commercial or mundane purposes, the stately art of the hieroglyph continued to be employed in sacred inscription. The language that the hieroglyphs conveyed was slow to change and evolve. The rise of the Indo-German tongues and their evolution would seem like speeded-up film compared to the development of Egyptian. But language is a living thing and does change, even in the context of a profoundly conservative society with a rooted respect for the great past. The hieroglyphic script, which once reflected the spoken language, came gradually to be overtaken by developments in speech and to be left behind.

Hieroglyphs were normally written from right to left, with the symbols facing the beginning of the row. Vertically arranged symbols have also been found, on the walls of buildings. *See also* SCRIBES.

Hittites

A dynamic and powerful people, centred in Anatolia, whose empire expanded southwards and came into conflict with that of Egypt during the NEW KINGDOM. Archaeology has revealed some of the first known diplomatic messages and peace treaties in official correspondence between Hittite and Egyptian monarchs.

homosexuality

The NEW KINGDOM text *The Story of HORUS and SETH* recounts an episode of mutual masturbation between the two gods, but there is little indication in the written or pictorial record of homosexuality. *The BOOK OF THE DEAD* encourages abstinence from homosexual acts. In a society founded on the concept of fertility, it may be that the cultural norms discouraged and repressed homosexuality without recourse to legal constraints. Certainly, in a culture as open in sexual matters as the Egyptian, if homosexuality were tolerated, one would expect to read a great deal more about it.

Honoured Ones

The group forming a king's closest advisers. They lived at court and formed a leading part of his retinue at all ceremonial occasions. Their functions would continue after the king's and their own deaths, as they received the right to have a tomb in proximity to the king's own and were provided with the materials to build and decorate it. *See also* COURT LIFE, PHARAOH'S DAY.

Horemheb

A NEW KINGDOM pharaoh, the last king of the EIGHTEENTH DYNASTY (ruled 1323–1295 BC). Although with no hereditary connection to his predecessor, he was a soldier who escorted TUTANKHAMUN on a demonstrative campaign in Palestine and who took the throne on the young king's death. Taking as his HORUS NAME 'powerful bull with wise decisions', he set about restoring order within the kingdom. The AMARNA PERIOD, with its religious controversies, had witnessed a form of iconoclasm in some temples of AMUN-RA, and Horemheb

Horus

made amends to the re-established deity. He began the HYPOSTYLE
HALL at KARNAK and constructed three pylons, using the stonework
of the nearby Aten temples. He superintended the introduction of
a conservative programme of worship and reformed the legal system, which had become excessively corrupt. He had no heir of his
own, and passed the crown to a fellow-general, RAMESES I.

Horus

The hawk-god, seen as the special protector of kings. Horus was
normally incorporated into the king's name, and the hawk motif
was widely used as a royal seal. Horus was the son and avenger
of OSIRIS, and was also known as 'son of RA' (a title also used by
kings). The oldest HIEROGLYPHICS to portray the concept of 'god'
use a falcon, indicating that the same word stood for both. Many
PRE-DYNASTIC localities had falcon-gods, and the history of Horus
is a palimpsest in which these many local origins come together
and continue to develop into the complicated entity of the classical Horus. At LETOPOLIS in the DELTA, there was an ancient cult of
a Horus known as *Hor-khent-irti*, 'Horus of the two eyes' (sun
and moon). The priests of HELIOPOLIS took this as the supreme
Horus and named four others as subordinate to him, 'the four
young ones who sit in the shadow of the lofty one' (the sons of
Horus). This was Horus the Elder, who was later to be assimilated in another Horus, Horus the Child, who was born to ISIS
and OSIRIS and who avenged the death of Osiris and became king
of Egypt, ancestor of all the pharaohs. Horus was thus a deity of
great significance, linked both to the light-giving sky and the
life-giving earth. His divine struggles found all sorts of practical
significances, as with the EYE OF HORUS, but his principal identification was with kings. There is a splendid statue of the FOURTH-

98

DYNASTY Pharaoh CHEPHREN with the Horus-falcon seated protectively on his shoulders.

Horus lock

A long twist of hair in a single lock on an otherwise close-shaven scalp, worn by CHILDREN of the nobility.

Horus name

The first of the royal set of names denoting a particular king; also the first in time. It associates the king with a particular aspect of the hawk-god.

houses

In the PRE-DYNASTIC PERIOD, houses were little more than tents: skins and textile spread over a wooden frame, or made of wattle and daub. These structures are preserved in early HIEROGLYPHICS. A headman's house would have a stockade around it, of sharpened sticks. By the THINITE PERIOD, wood-framed houses of a more substantial sort were built, with a mud-plaster outer covering. A pillared hall behind a portico was their main feature. By the MIDDLE KINGDOM there was an external stair leading to the roof and sometimes a proper second storey, however, most houses were single-storey. The hall remained the principal room of the house, where guests were received. There were private rooms for the master of the house, for his womenfolk and CHILDREN, and for guests. His servants lived outside the house but in their own meagre dwelling inside the fenced-off compound. Around the house would be ornamental gardens and flower beds. Shade and coolness were among the prime concern of the house-builder, and the garden would contain a pool surrounded by trees, overlooked from a broad portico supported by two rows of wooden pillars. A large house would have its own bakehouse, brewhouse, grain stores and workshops for weaving and CARPENTRY.

hygiene

The Egyptians set store by cleanliness, although their culture did not develop the bath house and its accompanying customs and rituals. They relied chiefly on cleansing oils, waxes and ointments to keep themselves clean and sweet-smelling. Men at least often kept their hair shaved off, except perhaps for one lock. At least partly for hygienic reasons, it was normal in both sexes to remove all bodily hair. *See also* SANITATION.

Hyksos

A dynasty of foreign rulers from Asia, including peoples from the Hitttite and Hurrian empires, who established themselves in the eastern DELTA around 1600 BC and controlled Lower and MIDDLE EGYPT for 100 years until Egyptian rule from THEBES was re-established. Their name is from the Egyptian *hekaw-khasut*, 'chiefs of foreign lands'. The struggle against the Hyksos was responsible for introducing many innovations to the Egyptians' methods of warfare, particularly the use of horses and chariots. Hyksos kings supplied the FIFTEENTH and Sixteenth Dynasties. Although there is little evidence of their having a dynamic foreign policy, the period does show an increase of Asiatic influence on Egyptian arts, crafts and religion, which was an enduring feature of the NEW KINGDOM despite its ebullient nationalist spirit.

hypostyle hall

A temple hall, supported by rows of COLUMNS, in which there were two levels of ceiling, supported by columns of different heights, creating a high central nave flanked by two lower aisles.

I

Iarsu *see* NINETEENTH DYNASTY; TWOSRE.

ideogram *see* HIEROGLYPHICS.

Imhotep
The VIZIER of the THIRD-DYNASTY Pharaoh Djoser, credited with commissioning the first PYRAMID, the Step Pyramid at Saqqara. He was a man of great consequence as an administrator and architect. He was deified in the course of the MIDDLE KINGDOM.

Inaros *see* PEDUBASTIS.

incense
Incense was used in temple and tomb ceremonies, where it created a mystical, perhaps even hallucinatory, atmosphere. It was burned in small decorative FAIENCE cups to give off an aromatic smoke.

inundation
The annual rise of the NILE in the August-November period, caused by the monsoon rains falling in the mountains of Ethiopia and southern SUDAN. Much land in the Nile Valley and the DELTA remained flooded for about 10 weeks. The levels varied from year to year, and there was a long and difficult period of low inundation during the OLD KINGDOM. At the first cataract the average rise was about 50 feet (15 metres); at the edge of the DELTA it was about 25 (7.5).

Inyotef I

The flood came in stages and was carefully observed and measured by the Egyptians. A green wave, laden with vegetable matter from the equatorial swamps, heralded the waters of the WHITE NILE. Two to four weeks later came the red wave, the waters of the BLUE NILE, stained by the red ferrous soil of the Ethiopian mountains and speeding up the pace of the inundation. The PYRAMID TEXTS of the SIXTH DYNASTY express the awe felt by the inhabitants at the spectacle: 'They tremble, who see Hapi when he beats his waves; but the meadows smile, the banks blossom, the offerings of the gods come down; men do homage; the hearts of the gods are lifted up.'

Inyotef I *see* ELEVENTH DYNASTY.

Isesi *see* FIFTH DYNASTY.

Isis

The prime goddess of the Egyptian pantheon, sister and wife of OSIRIS, mother of HORUS and a potent divinity in her own right. She is normally depicted in human form. Her origin was as the protective goddess of Per-hebit, north of Busiris in the DELTA. The ruins of her temple, the Iseium, still exist. Isis was famed for her magic skills, which enabled her to resurrect the re-assembled body of Osiris and make it copulate with her in order to produce Horus. Isis was often depicted as a midwife, and the moments of birth and death are both closely associated with her. Motherhood became a part of the Isis cult in the LATE PERIOD and gradually led to her being linked with the Mother Goddess of eastern religion. Her cult was still maintained at PHILAE long after the advent of Christianity.

itru *see* MEASUREMENT.

J

jewellery

This was a high ART in ancient Egypt, which was well endowed with precious stones and metals, and imported others. The jewellers used a wide range of materials, including agate, amethyst, beryl, calcite, carnelian, chalcedony, coral, garnet, jade, jasper, lapis lazuli, malachite, onyx, pearl, sardonyx and turquoise, with GOLD, SILVER and COPPER for settings. Gold itself was formed into ornamentation both by melting and casting and by hammering. Gold wire and gold leaf were extensively used. Perhaps the highest point of jewellery design was in the TWELFTH DYNASTY. Exquisite work was done on all sorts of personal adornments and accoutrements, including BRONZE hand mirrors whose reflective power associated them with the magic of the gods. *See also* ORNAMENTATION.

K

ka

A term used for the life force or spirit of an individual, which continued to reside inside the tomb, passing through the 'false door' into the chapel to receive offerings. One of the five elements constituting the human being, its HIEROGLYPHIC is two raised arms.

Ka'a *see* FIRST AND SECOND DYNASTIES.

Kamose *see* FIFTEENTH, SIXTEENTH AND SEVENTEENTH DYNASTIES.

Karnak

The site of a group of colossal temples, including the greatest of the Egyptian temples, that of AMUN-RA. The location is immediately north of THEBES, on the east bank of the NILE. The great temple complex was not all built at one time but was adapted and added to over no less than seven centuries. The granite-built sanctuary is the oldest portion and was complete before HYKSOS rule. In the reign of AMENOPHIS I, first king of the EIGHTEENTH DYNASTY, this was surrounded by a temple court, and in the reign of TUTHMOSIS I the grand facade was built in what became the standard Egyptian plan, two vast pylons of masonry, narrowing as they rose, crowned by wide curved cornices, another typically Egyptian feature. Between these two great structures was the gateway, at a lower level, also corniced. Two further such gateways were erected, one in front of the other. The hall between them was built in the reign of TUTHMOSIS III. Later kings added major sections, notably the great HYPOSTYLE HALL of COLUMNS, credited to SETHOS I and RAMESES II. There are 14 rows of PAPYRUS-bud columns, with two central rows of columns having capitals carved to resemble the open papyrus. These are 69 feet (21 metres) high and almost 12 feet (3.5 metres) round. Around 980 BC, during the TWENTY-SECOND Dynasty, the ninth and last pylon and the square forecourt in front of the hall of columns were added. The complete building is about 1200 feet (366 metres) long by 350 feet (107 metres) wide at its broadest and remains one of the largest buildings in the world. A ceremonial avenue lined by SPHINXES joined Karnak to THEBES, where further Eighteenth and NINETEENTH DYNASTY buildings rise, with OBELISKS, pylons, pillared courts and arcades, in honour of the Theban TRIAD, Amun-Ra, MUT and KHONSU. *See also* ARCHITECTURE, TEMPLE.

Keku Keket *see* COSMOLOGY.

Kenbet *see* LEGAL SYSTEM.

Kerma

A site in NUBIA, above the third cataract of the NILE, and centre of a local kingdom.

Khasekem

A warrior king of the Second Dynasty, conqueror of NUBIA, *c.*2700 BC. *See* FIRST AND SECOND DYNASTIES.

Khephren *see* CHEPHREN.

khet

A standard unit of MEASUREMENT of area, 100 square CUBITS.

Kheti I *and* II

Kheti I *and* II *see* Ninth and Tenth Dynasties.

Kheti III

The last king of the Tenth (Herakleopolitan) Dynasty (*see* Ninth and Tenth Dynasties) in the First Intermediate Period (2200–2040 BC); an active and effective king who drove the Asiatic colonizers out of the Nile Delta, reintroduced nomes as local government districts and renewed irrigation systems. His dynasty was, however, to be eclipsed by the Eleventh Dynasty (Theban), which ultimately triumphed in the long war with Herakleopolis that characterized the First Intermediate Period of Egyptian history.

Khnum

A ram-headed god whose cult was centred in the city of Elephantine. A potter, he was believed to have shaped the world and men upon his wheel in another version of the Creation myth.

Khonsu

A war-god of the later period, worshipped at Thebes, son of Amun and Mut.

Khufu *see* Cheops.

king *see* pharaoh.

king list

Lists of pharaohs' names inscribed on temple walls, as at Karnak and Abydos, or on papyrus, as in the Turin Canon. Although incomplete and sometimes mutually contradictory, they remain an important guide for the student of Egyptology.

kingship

The king, or pharaoh, was seen as a semi-divine figure. Metaphorically, and literally to many, he was son of Ra, the sun-god, and would ultimately rejoin his divine parent in the sky. His role on earth was to intercede on behalf of the country with the gods. To help make this effective, his life was encased in a set of ritual practices and religious ceremonies. He was high priest, above all others. But all strands of Egyptian life ultimately came together in the person of the king. He also had a decisive secular role; in his person the divine and the mortal came together. In the OLD KINGDOM period, it was believed that only the pharaoh, his immediate family and a few favoured others could attain to heaven. Justice was done in his name, and his word was law as well as sacred. The unchanging aspects of Egyptian life over centuries meant that kings were not required to be creative lawmakers or agents of change, which no doubt made AKHENATEN's religious revolution all the more shocking. But circumstances arose that required the king's decision or action, invasions, FAMINES, disputes between great men. Despite the official climate of adoration and fulsome praise, pharaohs were not immune from court plots, and several were assassinated as a result of conspiracies hatched in the harem, where rival queens were seeking the succession for their sons or nephews.

kiosk
A small, open-roofed chapel in which a god's statue was placed during a festival. One has been restored at KARNAK.

kohl *see* COSMETICS; ORNAMENTATION.

Koptos
Settlement on the River NILE, at the entrance to the Wadi Hammamet, with evidence of OLD and MIDDLE KINGDOM temples. It was particularly a cult centre of the fertility god MIN.

Kush

Kush
Egyptian term for NUBIA.

Kushite Dynasty *see* TWENTY-FIFTH DYNASTY.

L

land ownership

In principle, the king owned the land as well as everything else; others held it by his leave. From the Second Dynasty (*see* FIRST AND SECOND DYNASTIES) onwards, the king held a census every two years of land (immovable property) as well as movable goods. At this time there was still a distinction between the royal domain—the king's vineyards, orchards, fields, and woodlands—and the estates of private individuals; but as the royal power swiftly expanded, the entire area of Egypt came under royal control. The king granted land and could take it away. Land held under the king could be passed on by will but was subject to certain constraints. Under normal tenure, inherited land was divisible among all members of a family; but land given as a royal donation, to a successful soldier, for example, was transmissible without subdivision directly to the eldest son and therefore highly prized. A case is recorded in which one Mesmen appealed to the VIZIER at Heliopolis, and records of a land donation to his ancestor four hundred years previously were produced in his favour.

language

The language of the ancient Egyptians was brought by the Semitic peoples who moved into the Nile Valley from the Asiatic deserts.

Late Period

In its oldest forms it also shows traces of the African languages of the first inhabitants. It forms one of the languages of the Afro-Asiatic group (also known as the Hamito-Semitic group) that numbers over 200 living languages. The parent language of this vast and ancient group was spoken in the 7th millennium BC in Africa or the Middle East. Egyptian is now extinct, although in a much debased form, and heavily mixed with Greek, it can still be traced in COPTIC, a language that developed in Egypt from the 2nd century AD and is still used as a liturgical language by Christian communities in Egypt. It was in everyday use until the 18th–19th centuries. The language of modern Egypt is Arabic.

Late Period

(747–333 BC) The era between the THIRD INTERMEDIATE PERIOD and the MACEDONIAN DYNASTY. For nearly half of this period, Egypt was ruled by the Nubian or Kushite Dynasty (the TWENTY-FIFTH), when the former colony, which had become independent during the THIRD INTERMEDIATE PERIOD, displaying a vigour that Egypt itself had lost, overran and conquered its once predominant northern neighbour. This incursion first halted then stifled an Egyptian drive by the lords of SAIS in the western DELTA to unite the country under their own rule. Their descendants finally succeeded in 664 BC, when the Kushite kingdom fell before the invading Assyrians. The Saites formed the TWENTY-SIXTH DYNASTY, beginning as a puppet regime for the Assyrians. Under both the Kushite and the Saite kings, the country enjoyed a degree of stability and prosperity, given a firm central rule and a 'good Nile', Egypt could make a rapid recovery from any vicissitude, because of the size of her population and the potential for agricultural wealth if the state were well managed. The latter part of the Late Period was marked by two periods of Persian conquest, the first of which, 525–404 BC, signalled the end of the Saite revival. The period between 404 and the SECOND PERSIAN OCCUPATION in 343 was characterized by sporadic warfare and strenuous efforts to maintain alliances with the volatile Greek states in the almost constant effort to hold off the Persians. Despite this, especially under king NECTANEBO I, the last of the Egyptian PHARAOHS maintained the dignities, styles and practices of their predecessors, until the invasion of Artaxerxes III Ochos brought the Second Persian Occupation in 343 BC. This lasted for ten years until Alexander's destruction of the Persian empire. *See also* TWENTY-NINTH AND THIRTIETH DYNASTIES.

Late Pre-dynastic Period *see* PRE-DYNASTIC PERIOD.

legal system

At the administrative head of the legal system was the VIZIER, who dispensed and administered justice in the king's name. At a local level, each city possessed a council of elders, called the Saru in the OLD KINGDOM and the Kenbet from the MIDDLE KINGDOM onwards. This was an advisory body, and an active tribunal known as the DJADJAT was responsible to it for maintaining public order. Only minor cases could be dealt with locally, and anything of a serious nature was referred upwards to the Great Kenbet of MEMPHIS or that of THEBES. The vizier's was the supreme court. He alone could pronounce a death sentence, although only with the express permission of the pharaoh. His jurisdiction applied both to civil and criminal cases. In keeping with the whole Egyptian philosophy of life, law was given on a basis of precedent. The division between right and wrong was 'What Pharaoh loves' and 'What Pharaoh hates'. The vizier gave his judgements under very close scrutiny by his master, and a famous injunction by the Pharaoh TUTHMOSIS III to his vizier Rekhmara says, 'When a man is an official he should act according to the rules laid down for him. Happy is the man who does what he is told. Never swerve from the letter of justice . . . .' *See also* CRIME AND PUNISHMENT.

Letopolis

A settlement in LOWER EGYPT, a NOME capital on the west bank of the Rosetta arm of the NILE, an early source of the HORUS legend. Its deity was a mummified falcon.

Libya

The country to the west of the DELTA, exercising a strong influence on the western side and sometimes invading and overrunning it. There was traditional enmity between Egypt and Libya, extending back into PRE-DYNASTIC times, and warfare or punitive expeditions were frequent. Egypt also used Libyan mercenaries, and descendants of these provided the FIFTEENTH and Sixteenth Dynasties.

Libyan Dynasty *see* TWENTY-SECOND AND TWENTY-THIRD DYNASTIES.

lily

One of the symbols of the kingdom of UPPER EGYPT.

literature

The literature of the Egyptians is found in written form from the NINTH DYNASTY onwards, although there can be no doubt that, as with the legend of OSIRIS, there was a long-established oral tradition that related and passed on folk tales, folk humour and folk wisdom from generation to generation, both in literate and illiterate society. The survival of the oldest literary writings is often due to copies made by scribes in later periods. OLD KINGDOM literature is primarily religious, the expression particularly of the priests of HELIOPOLIS. The PYRAMID TEXTS fall into this category. Other inscriptions of a less ritualistic sort are occasionally found in the Old Kingdom tombs at MEMPHIS, including short fragments of songs or popular sayings. PAPYRUS sources are found from the FIRST INTERMEDIATE PERIOD, when the anxieties of the time prompted some scribes to put their thoughts down in writing and to comment sourly or pessimistically on the spirit of the age.

There are several long stories from the MIDDLE KINGDOM, including *The Tale of* SINUHE, *The Tale of the* ELOQUENT PEASANT and *The Tale of the Shipwrecked Sailor*. These stories have a strong element of fantasy. From the same period comes the new religious literature, on sarcophagi, temple walls and papyri, spreading the previously esoteric formulae that enabled all good people to enter the UNDERWORLD. From this time also come collections of proverbs and wise maxims. Few poems have been preserved from this period, apart from a collection of hymns in praise of the Pharaoh Sesostris III. Altogether, the MIDDLE KINGDOM remnants suggest a wide variety of literature, both narrative, lyrical and didactic.

The writings of the NEW KINGDOM are more realistic in tone and sometimes display a brutally down-to-earth attitude. They include such stories as *The Tale of the Doomed Prince*, *The Tale of the Two Brothers*, *The Tale of Truth and Falsehood*, *The Voyage of Wenamon*, and *The Tale of* HORUS *and* SETH. From this period we also have poetry in the form of AKHENATEN's hymns to the sun-god Ra-Aten, a love-poem cycle similar to the Song of Songs, and sundry official poems addressed to PHARAOHS and gods. The counter-reformation of ATUM also has its hymns to the god.

Lower Egypt

A favourite form of writing for the Egyptians was the collection of maxims, giving guidance on how to lead a life of such poise and virtue that would ensure an easy passage at the trial of Osiris. Egyptian prose writing, even at its most creative, has a stilted and repetitive feeling, with a formulaic quality and an artificiality of style and tone that were accepted and appreciated by the contemporary reader in a way with which we find it hard to empathize. But writing, like every other form of ART and craft, was expected to serve the purposes of the state. The works are anonymous, following fixed forms and canons and produced for specific purposes. Literature was not for its own sake, it was essentially utilitarian.

Lower Egypt

The area of the Nile DELTA between MEMPHIS and the Mediterranean coast. Below Memphis, the Nile splits into two great arms, the western (Rosetta) arm and the eastern (Damietta) arm. The area between them, despite its marshiness and propensity to flood at the time of the INUNDATION (although here the rise was far less because of the width and number of the streams), was densely inhabited from an early period. It was later subdivided into 17 NOMES, each of which indicates the presence of a distinct tribal group or clan with its own chieftain and its own protective deity. Much of Egyptian religion was evolved in this region, with major cult centres such as BUSIRIS (for ANZTI/OSIRIS), BUBASTIS (BASTET), BUTO (the cobra goddess of the same name), HELIOPOLIS (RA), LETOPOLIS (HORUS the Elder).

Apart from Memphis, which was a later settlement despite its eventual status as capital, its major centres were the cities of TANIS, on the eastern side, and SAIS, on the western, as well as the cult centres. Both Tanis and Sais, as well as Memphis, were to provide Egypt with royal dynasties. Lower Egypt, open to the sea on its north front, and with empty desert stretching to LIBYA on the east and to Palestine in the west, was always more open to influence and attack from outside than was UPPER EGYPT. The initiative in the joining of the two kingdoms came from here, and the archaeological evidence of PRE-DYNASTIC times indicates the spreading of advanced culture up the Nile Valley rather than downstream. In the NEW KINGDOM and LATE PERIOD its population became increasingly mixed, with strong influxes of Libyans, Greeks, Jews and Assyrians.

Luxor

Site in UPPER EGYPT, on the east bank of the NILE, immediately south of, and often equated with, THEBES. The name comes from Arabic and refers to Roman camps built on the site. AMENOPHIS III built a splendid temple here, partly on top of older buldings, which was enlarged and decorated by later kings, forming a uniquely impressive linked site with the temple of AMUN-RA at Thebes.

M

Maat

The goddess of truth. She presided over the judgement of the dead, which controlled entry to the UNDERWORLD. Human-faced, she is a later addition to the pantheon.

Macedonian Dynasty

The dynasty, 332–304 BC, that followed the Thirtieth Dynasty (*see* TWENTY-NINTH AND THIRTIETH DYNASTIES), with which the numbering system ceases. The Persian satrap of Egypt resigned his satrapy to ALEXANDER THE GREAT, with the consent of the people, as expressed by the ORACLE of AMUN-RA at THEBES, which hailed Alexander as Master of the Universe. The Macedonians, Alexander himself (ruled Egypt 333–323 BC), Philip Arrhidaeus (323–316 BC) and Alexander IV (316–304 BC), all preserved the forms of Egyptian life and society. Like the Persian empire, Alexander's was too vast and disparate for it to live under one set of laws. Egypt, with its immemorial tradition and the inherent stability of its systems, could function as a state within the greater empire. The key to this lay with the priesthood. Religion and the AFTERLIFE remained an obsession with the Egyptians, and the gods and their priests remained a constant factor in the life of the country, whoever held the crown. In the peace that followed Alexander's conquest, the priesthood kept or renewed its privileges, and temple reconstruction and temple-building went on at a rapid pace.

magic

The Egyptians made some distinction between magic and religion. The household of the PHARAOH contained magicians as well as priests. The priestly function was to venerate the gods and make supplications. The magician's function was to use his wiles to circumvent the gods' will or to compel them towards certain actions. His power, too, devolved from the gods themselves, particularly from ISIS, the great magician who resurrected OSIRIS, and THOTH, the keeper of records, including divine spells. Talismans and spells were the armoury of the magician. The talismans, AMULETS of wood, metal, clay or pottery, depict HIEROGLYPHIC signs for such attributes as long life, health, strength, fertility, beauty, etc. They are linked to the power of a particular god, and a spell would be recited to increase their efficacy. The magician could exorcise a malign spirit that was causing illness or misfortune if he knew its name (see NAMES). The magicians were close observers of the stars and made prophecies relating to their conjunctions. Much of the later continuing tradition of 'black magic' stems from the pratices of the Egyptian magicians, who used wax figures of their intended victims and created love potions and elixirs of life. Even Pharaoh Rameses III had to take protective action against a magician who 'had stolen the secret books of the king, to bewitch and destroy the people of the court'. The 'wise men' had to be taken account of. They were numbered among the king's advisers, and the king himself would proclaim that he had been taught the secret knowledge of things by THOTH and that he, like Thoth, was also the Great Magician.

Maidum

A site on the west bank of the NILE, about 30 miles (50 kilometres) south of SAQQARA, where the Pharaoh SNOFRU of the FOURTH DYNASTY erected a PYRAMID, which, initially a step pyramid like that of Djoser, was altered to form a uniform-slope pyramid cased in limestone masonry, the first of its type. Maidum was also the site of the first valley temple, a temple separated from the pyramid complex, at which the dead king's FUNERARY rites were carried out.

Manetho

An Egyptian priest from the time of Greek rule (around 250 BC), who compiled a kind of history of Egypt together with a list of kings and dynasties. Lost in the original, his text is known through other writers' quotations and comments. It has been a vexation almost as much as a blessing to Egyptologists, since so much of it has been lost and so much of what survives is flimsy legend and obviously false or misleadingly phrased information, such as his reference to 'seventy kings in seventy days' during the FIRST INTERMEDIATE PERIOD.

Mariette, Auguste

(1821–81) French Egyptologist who became Keeper of Monuments to the Egyptian government. He excavated the SPHINX and uncovered many other monuments.

marriage customs

Marriage was an important institution in Egyptian life, and on the whole, among the general population, it seems to have been a voluntary affair rather than a matter of purchase or arrangement. There was no special wedding ceremony, no dowry or bride price, and no marriage contract was necessary; such contracts often came later in a marriage, when impending death or perhaps divorce meant that assets had to be counted and apportioned. As with the royal families, it appears that there was no bar against incestuous marriages. Men could have more than one wife, but the status of the chief wife was protected by law. In practice, the vast bulk of the population was monogamous, if only for economic reasons; very few men could support more than one wife, especially as they may have had other female relations to support. Husband and chief wife lived together on equal terms, and she had considerable rights of her own. Her eldest son, even if not the eldest son of the husband, would normally be the chief heir. Divorce was provided for, and seems to have been as relatively unregulated as marriage, apart from the property aspect. Husbands could repudiate a wife whom they regarded as unsatisfactory, and there is some evidence to suggest that wives had a reciprocal right, although much less likely to exercise it because of social custom and the difficulty of maintaining an independent existence. Adultery was considered a serious crime, particularly in women, but despite various accounts of severe penalties like nose-slitting or even death, it was most commonly settled by divorce, and an adulterous wife might lose her legal rights to a share of the family goods. *See also* WOMEN.

masonry

The Egyptians became highly skilled stonemasons at an early stage, although the conservatism of design meant that their skill showed itself in perfection of technique rather than in inventiveness. Their tools were made of the hardest stone or of COPPER, with BRONZE tools developed in the course of the NEW KINGDOM.

Maspero, Gaston

With such rudimentary equipment they cut, chiselled and shaped huge blocks of stone and fitted them together with minute precision. They knew the principle of the arch but never employed it, sticking to the ancient column-and-lintel style of the first structures. A distinctive characteristic of the Egyptian stonemason was to cut some of his blocks at an oblique rather than a vertical angle. This was not a decorative feature, as all temples were coated with a thin layer of white plaster, concealing the stone from view.

Maspero, Gaston

(1846–1916) French Egyptologist, discoverer of the PYRAMID TEXTS. He served as Director of the Antiquities service, made valuable discoveries at SAQQARA and DAHSHUR, and was instrumental in saving the royal mummies at THEBES from tomb robbers.

mastaba

A structure of brick, later of stone, with decorative niches, to indicate and to seal a tomb. The name is from an Arabic word, meaning 'bench', which was how the mastabas seemed to the Arab workers employed by 19th-century archaeologists. The original mastabas, in the FIRST Dynasty, were solid. In the SECOND (and later) Dynasties they became steadily larger and more elaborate, with a room or rooms inside; and eventually a whole group of intersecting rooms above a substantial underground plan. By the late Second Dynasty, mastabas were of sufficient size to prompt the notion of the step PYRAMID, with the mastaba as its base storey.

mathematics

Like many other aspects of intellectual life, mathematics in Egypt appears to have been developed in the PRE-DYNASTIC and THINITE PERIODS, and to have progressed little from the period of the PYRA-

MIDS. With their aversion to speculative and abstract thought, mathematics was not a congenial subject to the Egyptians, who pursued it not for its own sake but for the practical application it had to their needs. This related chiefly to ARCHITECTURE and building. Like all subjects that had to be taught, mathematics was in the province of the priests, who were fearful of making their knowledge too widely known, since it was perceived as magic. The mathematical formulae were more akin to spells than general truths to them. The decimal system was employed, with multiples of 100 up to 1 million. There was no zero. *See also* MEASUREMENT.

mayor

The headman of a town or settlement, although, of course, he was appointed, very often as a hereditary official, not elected. He would be among the wealthiest inhabitants and had local powers to maintain order and settle disputes. Much of his duties would involve preparing for visits from more important state officials and ensuring that they were suitably lodged and entertained.

measurement

The social organization of the NILE Valley was dependent on a universal system of measurement. The standard measures were taken from the human form. The unit of short measure, used by painters and sculptors in particular, was the foot. The unit of long measure was the CUBIT, which subdivided into two spans, six hands or 24 fingers. The standard cubit was about 46 centimetres, with the royal cubit being some four centimetres longer. Longer distances were measured by the itru, around 5,000 cubits. The royal surveyors measured land in squares of 100 royal cubits (the KHET). The standard unit of capacity was the henu, of about one-third of a litre (11 fluid ounces). The basic unit of weight, the DEBEN, was about $3^1/_4$ ounces (91 grams).

medicine

Occupying a position somewhere between empirical science and superstitious magic, medicine was greatly respected, and Egyptian doctors had a high reputation in the ancient world. Medical inscriptions date back to the MIDDLE KINGDOM, although they often claim to be copies of documents originating from the OLD KINGDOM. Given the Egyptian respect for traditional knowledge, this may well be true, or it may be a means of giving authority to more recent treatments. Medicine, like every other form of knowledge, lived under the umbrella of the priesthood. Early doctors appear to have been priests chiefly of Serket and of NEITH. Temples had their herb gardens to provide a supply of medicaments, and among the gods who sponsored the art of curing were RA-ATUM himself, Neith (whose temple at SAIS had a medical school adjacent to the school of the Wise Magicians) and ANUBIS. The most reliable and effective medical treatments were those that were applied to external solutions. The Egyptians were good bone-setters. They also practised amputation successfully. Wounds and cuts were treated with bandages and poultices impregnated with antiseptic herbs and ointments. Internal illness was far more of a mystery, and the doctor reverted to spells and potions, as his successors would do in other lands, too, for centuries after the end of the Egyptian kingdom. These frequently involved the use of odd products like lizard's blood, the excrement of various animals and mother's milk. Incantations accompanied the administration of the medicine. Prescriptions were adapted to the age of the patient and the time of the year: a medicine that cured in the first month of summer might not do so in the second. Doctors knew the importance of the heart but had a strange ignorance of the softer organs of the human body, considering that their own society also practised a sophisticated form of embalming that involved the removal of the viscera. But the doctors were not embalmers, and the embalmers were not doctors.

A number of papyri on medical topics have come down to us, showing among other things that the Egyptians were students of gynaecology. Much of this interest centred on infertility and its supposed cures, often bizarre if not harmful, and again there was no serious anatomical study. Cosmetic medicine was also extensively practised. One surviving treatise is entitled *Book for Turning an Old Man into a Youth of Twenty*. Medical materials were chiefly plant-based, and the Egyptians knew the uses of castor oil, mandragora, dill, cumin, hartshorn and coriander, among others. HERODOTUS noted the degree of specialization among Egyptian doctors, as healers of the eyes, the head, the belly, and so on, and observed, 'The Egyptians look after their health with emetics and purgatives, and clear themselves out for three days running, once a month, considering that all the ailments of men come from the food they eat.' *See also* DISEASE, HYGIENE, SANITATION, TEMPLE.

Medinet Habu

The site of numerous temples on the west bank of the NILE, facing THEBES, and in the vast funerary region that includes Malqata and DEIR EL BAHRI. It includes the MORTUARY TEMPLE of TUTANKHAMUN (EIGHTEENTH DYNASTY) and the great palace-temple of RAMESES III (TWENTY-SECOND DYNASTY).

Medjay

A desert tribe from whom the Egyptians recruited soldiers, including internal guards: an early application of the principle that a district should not provide its own policemen.

Memphis

Close to modern Cairo, and strategically placed at the apex of the Nile DELTA, ancient MEMPHIS was the capital during the period of the THIRD to the SIXTH DYNASTIES (2980–2475 BC), the most brilliant period of the OLD KINGDOM. It was founded on a reclaimed flood plain by AHA at the start of the FIRST DYNASTY as the 'city of the white wall'. As a new foundation it had no tutelary god from prehistoric times and took over PTAH from a nearby settlement. It was the prestige of HELIOPOLIS, north of Memphis, that drew the kings to move steadily northwards, incorporating the name of RA into their titles. The name changed to Memphis under the reign of PEPY I, who established a new royal district and called it Menefer, 'good harbour', later transliterated into Greek as Memphis. Always a place of high prestige, Memphis became capital again with the TWELFTH DYNASTY and again with the HYKSOS invaders of the FIFTEENTH DYNASTY. The location of Memphis as a point controlling both the DELTA and the Valley made it attractive to invaders. Libyan, Nubian, Assyrian and Persian armies all headed for Memphis, and the captor of Memphis was in effect the captor of Egypt. When Cambyses took Memphis in the first Persian conquest, the reigning PHARAOH, Psammetichus II, committed suicide. The funerary sites of Memphis, SAQQARA and DAHSHUR are among the richest and most splendid of ancient Egypt.

Mendes

A site on the southern side of the DELTA, NOME capital and capital of the Thirtieth Dynasty kings (*see* TWENTY-NINTH AND THIRTIETH DYNASTIES).

Meni *see* AHA.

Menkaure *see* MYCERINUS.

Mentuhotpe II

ELEVENTH-DYNASTY king (ruled 2040–2009 BC) and first king of the MIDDLE KINGDOM, who came to the throne of the Theban kingdom and later extended his kingship over all Egypt with the military defeat of the Herakleopolitans. To mark this he took a new title, Nebhepetre ('son of RA'), and later took a new HORUS NAME, Sematawy ('he who unifies the two lands'). Setting up his capital at THEBES, he restored many of the functions and systems of the OLD KINGDOM, including the VIZIERSHIP, and built numerous temples, including that of HATHOR at Gebelein, and added to the complex of buildings serving OSIRIS at ABYDOS. After a lengthy reign he died in 2009 BC, leaving a far more united and prosperous kingdom behind him. His tomb is in the rock cliffs of DEIR EL BAHRI.

Mentuhotpe III

ELEVENTH-DYNASTY king (ruled 2009–1997 BC). The son of MENTUHOTPE II, he was another strong king who continued internal reforms, consolidated the defences of the DELTA region and sent a large trading expedition to PUNT.

Mentuhotpe IV *see* ELEVENTH DYNASTY.

Merenra *see* PEPY I; SIXTH DYNASTY; WENI.

merkhet

A surveying instrument used by the Egyptians in laying out the ground for a temple or PYRAMID.

metal-working

On the wall of a passage leading to the PYRAMID temple of the

Middle Egypt

Sixth-Dynasty King Teti at Saqqara there is the relief depiction of a metalworking shop. The metals being worked are electrum, 'white gold', an alloy of GOLD and SILVER, and COPPER. Four men are shown hammering sheets of metal with stone hammers. Two others are blowing through long tubes to raise the fire under a crucible of electrum. Another scene shows a craftsman shaping or polishing a metal bowl round a wooden modelling core, while others are putting the finishing touches to handled water jugs. Other scenes show the weighing of metal ingots and the sharpening of an adze blade. Such establishments were not large and were workshops rather than factories, employing a relatively small number of skilled craftsmen. There was a royal monopoly on the working of metal, and such workshops would be under the administration of an official ultimately responsible through a long hierarchic chain to the VIZIER.

The Egyptians knew iron at first only through meteorite fragments, which would be viewed as god-sent and used only for sacred ornamentation, and the occasional gift from a foreign king. COPPER remained the foundation of Egyptian metalwork, although by the NEW KINGDOM it was being alloyed with tin to make BRONZE. Tin was not accessible in Egypt, and bronze remained in limited use. Copper was used in many different ways. Copper pipes were used to carry water, and even drainage, and many of the jugs, bowls and drinking vessels of the wealthy were made of it.

Middle Egypt

A geographical term applied to the Nile Valley between ASYUT and Cairo.

Middle Kingdom

The period of the ELEVENTH to the FOURTEENTH DYNASTIES (2040–

1675 BC), a distinctive epoch between the chaotic conditions of the
FIRST INTERMEDIATE PERIOD and the first instance of foreign rule.
With a succession of strong and determined kings in its first two
dynasties, the early Middle Kingdom represents perhaps the peak
of Egyptian prosperity and internal security. It was a time of rela-
tive peace, in which trading overseas and overland was widely practised. In the conversion of the FAIYUM region from marshland to
irrigated farmland, a vast public work was achieved whose purpose owes nothing either to death or defence, which hitherto had
been the principal objects of such expense. Not that funerary AR-
CHITECTURE was neglected, as the Middle Kingdom PHARAOHS once
again had the resources to build PYRAMIDS. In this and in many other
ways they looked back to the time of the OLD KINGDOM for inspiration and example. They wanted to feel that they were perpetuating
the ancient traditions of the country; that there was a continuing
link back to the days of such figures as SNOFRU and IMHOTEP, both
of whom were deified during the Middle Kingdom. It was a rich
period for Egyptian literature, in some repects a 'classical' period,
in which the writers praised the circumstances of their own time
and looked back into the heroic past for parallels or examples. But
it was also in the Middle Kingdom that the great mythological accounts, such as *The Tale of* HORUS *and* SETH, were set down. The
later dynasties were less distinguished, but the continuity of religion, culture and work went on almost changelessly through a succession of pharaohs of whom little is known. *See also* ELEVENTH TO
FOURTEENTH DYNASTIES.

Middle Pre-dynastic Period *see* PRE-DYNASTIC PERIOD.

military organization

In the OLD KINGDOM, the isolation of Egypt was such that an

organized ARMY was not normally required. At need, an army of sorts could be levied from the peasantry. During the FIRST INTERMEDIATE PERIOD internal warfare as well as greater contact with other states brought about a swift increase in the number of trained soldiers and a regular army came into being. Many of the soldiers were mercenaries from other lands; the Egyptian tradition and lifestyle was anything but militaristic, and they did not take to warfare with any enthusiasm. By the time the NEW KINGDOM had established an Egyptian empire, however, the army was very large and possessed considerable prestige, aided by the efforts of the priesthood to instil enthusiasm for the cause of Egyptian arms.

Min

A fertility god whose cult centre was KOPTOS. Popular especially in MIDDLE EGYPT, and with many chapels attached to the temples of other gods, he was portrayed as a rotund figure with a large penis. Statues and charms featuring Min were very common.

Mineptah *see* NINETEENTH DYNASTY.

Mitanni

An Indo-European people of relatively advanced skills in social organization and in warfare. Coming from farther east, they imposed themselves on the Hurrian kingdom in Mesopotamia as an aristocratic ruling class, and confrontation with Egypt followed. Egyptian relations with Mitanni were to fluctuate violently between savage war and peaceful alliance. Under TUTHMOSIS III the Egyptians defeated the Mitanni on their own territory and put them under tribute. The Mitanni, faced with a nearer and more hostile kingdom, as the HITTITE power increased, sought friendship and alliance with Egypt in its phase of Tuthmosid imperial power.

Montu
The tutelary god of THEBES, later overshadowed and absorbed by AMUN-RA.

mortuary temple
The temple in which the religious cult of a dead king was celebrated. Statues of the deceased would be placed in its sanctum, together with those of gods with whom he had been especially associated. Its store rooms would contain votive offerings and the walls were decorated with testaments to his greatness and his fitness for the AFTERLIFE. It was to the mortuary temple that the KA of the dead king or queen would come to inspect and receive the offerings placed there by the priests of the cult and, on anniversaries, by the royal successors. In the OLD and MIDDLE KINGDOMS, the mortuary temple was immediately adjacent to the PYRAMID or tomb. In the NEW KINGDOM period it was in a separate location.

mummification
The first evidence of this practice, so firmly identified with ancient Egypt, is on a tablet from the reign of Djer, last of the FIRST-DYNASTY kings, although in popular legend the first Egyptian to be embalmed and consequently reincarnated was OSIRIS himself. The word 'mummy' comes from the Arabic *mumiyah*, meaning bitumen. Until the popularizing of the Osiris cult, mummification was only practised on kings and those closest to them, but from the MIDDLE KINGDOM onwards it was made available to all who could afford it. The business of embalming and mummify-

ing was managed by a special guild of craftsmen, recognized by law. The dry sandy soil of Egypt had a natural tendency to preserve dead bodies, allowing the fluids to drain away and preventing the flesh from rotting. In the PRE-DYNASTIC millennia, the inhabitants of Egypt must have become well aware of this and regarded the preservation of a corpse as something natural and, by extension, desirable, willed by the gods. When their burial practice became more elaborate than the simple earthen pit, it must have soon become apparent that in a stone-lined cell beneath a MASTABA the process of desiccation did not happen and putrefaction was much more likely. Embalming and mummification emerged as the answer to this problem. After death, the corpse was taken to a special house of purification. It was laid out on a slab, and the brain was removed, drawn out through the nose aperture with a hook after a process of maceration. A FLINT knife was used to cut open the left side, and the internal organs, stomach, liver, intestines, etc, were extracted. The maker of the initial cut might run away, with the other undertakers in mock pursuit, in a ritualized enactment of guilt and expiation. The soft parts were given separate treatment; embalmed, wrapped and placed in the four so-called 'CANOPIC JARS'. The heart was left in the body, as it had to be weighed on the entry into the UNDERWORLD. The body was then packed in NATRON for from 35 to 70 days to dry it out. Pieces of material were then soaked in gums, sweetened with herbs and placed in the abdominal cavity. The wound made by the dissector was covered with a plaque that conferred the protection of the four sons of HORUS. The body was then ritually cleaned and purified before the wrapping began. Each individual member, including the fingers and the penis in the case of males, was wrapped in linen, over which went a piece of material that covered the torso. Selected charms and AMULETS were placed at particular parts of the body or inserted between the layers of bandaging. The number of layers varied. The mummy of TUTANKHAMUN had 16. Finally, a mask was prepared to go over the face, and the mummy was ready for its interment. *See* FUNERARY PRACTICE.

music

Music was present in Egyptian life in many different ways. Workers in the fields sang folk songs and love songs to traditional tunes. Many work activities were carried out to a strong rhythm, produced by percussion, rowing, marching, pulling and heaving. Music played a large part in social life. It was an essential accompaniment to the many feasts and parties, and professional musicians were well paid. Musicians were often women; indeed, perhaps there were more women musicians than there were male ones. Percussion was basic to the orchestra, with various types of rattles and clappers in use as well as drums of different sizes and construction. There were also wind and stringed instruments, forms of the flute, clarinet and harp. In the NEW KINGDOM period, the lute and the lyre were brought in from Asia, with foreign performers. There was also an early form of bagpipe. Temples used music to please the gods, who loved feasts at least as much as mortal men did, and there were corps of sacred musicians, singers and dancers. A number of high-ranking women became religious singers. Among the gods, music was mostly a perquisite of the female deities, with HATHOR in particular closely identified with the sistrum, an instrument whose use was restricted to women. It was a rattle-type instrument with a long handle, decorated with the cow-head of the goddess. Music was also associ-

Mut

ated with the brothel, and prostitutes are often depicted with a
lute or lyre. In those temples where sacred prostitutes practised,
there was no dividing line between the prostitute, the dancer and
the musician.

Mut

Wife to AMUN-RA, the goddess-mother, a vulture-headed goddess local to THEBES and so given this elevated status and provided there with a splendid temple but little worshipped elsewhere.

Mycerinus *or* Menkaure

A FOURTH-DYNASTY (2625–2510 BC) PHARAOH, builder of the
smallest of the three PYRAMIDS of GIZA.

N

names

Egyptian gradually ceased to be a living language after the Roman occupation. During the period of the Greek kings, Greek had become the official language, and many Egyptian names come to us through their Greek form, taken from the lists left by MANETHO. Since, in Egyptian writing, the consonants in a word only were set down, the vowel sound is sometimes a matter of conjecture. Even so short a name as that of RA is spelled Re by some writers. By the time they have been rendered again from Greek to English, they are likely to be phonetically and alphabetically remote from the Egyptian original. The pronunciation of Egyptian can only be guessed at. Consequently, different Egyptologists have spelt names in different ways, and there has been much debate and argument about how a 'correct' orthography for ancient Egyptian names could be set up. The picture is further complicated by the number of names each PHARAOH possessed. In recent years, there has been movement towards a degree of standardization, with the former -en ending now much more often seen as -on or -un. Since the Hellenized (Greek) forms are the most established and most widely found in the literature on ancient Egypt, these chiefly are used in this dictionary with cross-references to alternative forms when these are relatively common, as with Tuthmosis and Thotmes, Sesostris and Senusret, and others.

naming

The possession of a name was of literally vital importance to the Egyptians. A baby was given its name immediately after birth, so that it should have a name even if it died in post-birth trauma. There is a close connection between the power of naming and the magic element in Egyptian religious thought. Not to have a name was to be in a form of limbo. Knowledge of a name might confer some secret power over that named person. To obliterate the name inscribed on a king's CARTOUCHE was to jeopardize his continuing existence in the AFTERLIFE. For such reasons, the naming of PHARAOHS was a complicated business, hedged about with precautions. In the early dynasties, the king was given three names. These were later added to as the concept of the god-king grew. By the NINTH DYNASTY the final form was established. The names of the NINETEENTH-DYNASTY king RAMESES II were as follows. His HORUS NAME was 'mighty bull, beloved of justice'. His Lord of the Two Lands (*nbty*) name was 'defender of Egypt, binder of foreign lands'. His GOLDEN HORUS NAME was 'rich in years, great in victories'. His king of Upper and LOWER EGYPT name (also known as the TWO LADIES NAME) was 'rich in the justice of RA, chosen of Ra' (this was his coronation name, shown on the first CARTOUCHE designating him). His Son of Ra name was 'beloved of AMUN, Ramses' (his birth name, inscribed on the second CARTOUCHE designating him). By contrast, most ordinary Egyptians had only a single personal name, perhaps with a reference to the father added.

naos

A shrine or niche in the innermost part of a temple or chapel, where a divine statue was placed.

Napata
The capital city of NUBIA, situated below the third cataract of the NILE. Following the end of the Nubian Dynasty (the TWENTY-FIFTH DYNASTY), the capital moved farther into the hinterland, at Meroe.

Naqadal Period *see* PRE-DYNASTIC PERIOD.

Narmer *see* AHA.

natron
A mineral produced by combining sodium carbonate and bicarbonate and naturally found as deposits of sesquicarbonate of soda, this was an important element in MUMMIFICATION as a drying and an antiseptic agent. It had many other uses, including the manufacture of FAIENCE and glassware, and in soldering metal. It was used with salt to preserve meat, and, when mixed with oil and scented unguents, produced a kind of soap.

Necho I *and* **II** *see* TWENTY-SIXTH DYNASTY.

necropolis
An area set aside for tombs (Greek: 'city of death'). Tomb areas were generally to the west of cities and settlements, as the west was seen as the direction in which the dead travelled, towards the sunset.

Nectanebo I
PHARAOH (ruled 380–362 BC) of the final dynastic period, the Thirtieth (*see* TWENTY-NINTH AND THIRTIETH DYNASTIES), whose reign was dominated by efforts to keep the Persians from re-claiming Egypt as a satrapy. There was intensive diplomacy and shifting of alliances between Egypt and the Greek states, with Egypt in a very weak negotiating position. Nectanebo organized

defences against invasion, but a Greek-Persian fleet evaded these by attacking the western DELTA. The way to MEMPHIS was open, but they delayed, waiting for Persian reinforcements, and, aided by the July INUNDATION and the Egyptians' mastery of the waterways, Nectanebo was able to drive them out. Even at this time, the traditional pharaonic activities were maintained. During Nectanebo's 18-year rule, a vast programme of temple restoration was carried out. He also began the temple of ISIS at PHILAE, and made endowments to temples at SAIS, EDFU and elsewhere.

Nectanebo II

The last Egyptian-born king of ancient Egypt (ruled 360–343 BC). Displaced by the SECOND PERSIAN OCCUPANCY, he retreated southwards and eventually took refuge in NUBIA, where he maintained a government in exile for few years. *See* TWENTY-NINTH AND THIRTIETH DYNASTIES.

Neferefre

PHARAOH of the OLD KINGDOM, FIFTH DYNASTY (2510–2460 BC). His MORTUARY TEMPLE at ABUSIR was excavated in the 1980s AD and revealed a large collection of PAPYRUS scrolls, inscribed plaques, statues of the king's prisoners and sculptures of the king himself.

Neferirkare

PHARAOH of the OLD KINGDOM, FIFTH DYNASTY (2510–2460 BC). In his tomb at ABUSIR was found one of the most valuable collections of papyri relating to the OLD KINGDOM.

Nefertari *see* EIGHTEENTH DYNASTY.

Nefertiti

Queen consort of AKHENATEN. Her fine painted portrait bust (in the Berlin Museum) has been very well preserved. Nefertiti, who may have been of Asiatic origin, perhaps from MITANNI, shared her husband's enthusiasm for the worship of ATEN. When his failure to sustain the cult compelled him to compromise with the priests of AMUN, she separated from him to live in a house named 'fortress of the Aten' at AKHETATEN. After Akhenaten's death, she asked the HITTITE king to send her one of his sons as a husband. There may have been an ambitious dynastic and religious scheme behind this, but the prince was killed by agents of the priests of Amun-Ra on his way to Egypt; and with the eradication of Aten-worship, Nefertiti fell into obscurity.

Neith
A goddess whose origins go into the PRE-DYNASTIC PERIOD. She was a huntress and a major goddess of the TWENTY-SIXTH DYNASTY, which was centred on her cult centre of SAIS, in the western DELTA.

nemes headdress
A royal headdress, made of cloth, knotted at the back and with two prominent side lappets.

Neolithic Period
This era of human development begins at the end of the 7th millennium BC. It leads in to the PRE-DYNASTIC PERIOD of Egyptian history, over a period of some 2000 years, a time of significant cultural development. Although stone was by far the most important source of tools and weapons, metals were gradually being introduced. Society evolved with settled agricultural practice, based on crop growing and animal husbandry.

Nephthys
An ancient but relatively unimportant goddess, sister and wife

Neuserre

of SETH but nevertheless devoted to both OSIRIS and ISIS. She assisted Isis to find the body of Osiris.

Neuserre *see* FIFTH DYNASTY; FUNERARY PRACTICE.

New Kingdom

From around 1552–1070 BC, the period of the EIGHTEENTH to the TWENTIETH DYNASTIES. Some sources take it as lasting until the end of dynastic Egypt (*see* LATE PERIOD). The New Kingdom showed the underlying resilience of Egyptian institutions after the SECOND INTERMEDIATE PERIOD, with its rule by the foreign HYKSOS kings. Under a succession of strong kings, Egypt was turned into the most powerful state in the world, its frontiers extending from NUBIA to the Euphrates. Wealth poured in from client kingdoms in the form of GOLD, luxury goods and slaves. International diplomacy developed, and many aspects of life and ART were influenced by Asian examples. For the first time, there was intermarriage between kings of Egypt and foreign princesses. The internal situation was less secure than at the high point of the MIDDLE KINGDOM, with tensions between the kings and the powerful high priests of AMUN-RA, reflected in the religious controversy that reached its height when AKHENATEN attempted to supplant Amun-Ra with ATEN. The New Kingdom's ARCHITECTURE was as ambitious as its foreign policy and reached a peak of grandiloquence under RAMESES II. The final century of the New Kingdom was one of gradual decline after the brilliant early period, and it ended with Egypt's prestige at a low ebb and the kingdom itself again divided in two. *See also* NINETEENTH DYNASTY.

Nile

The great river, whose BLUE NILE branch rises in the mountains of Equatorial Africa, and whose longer WHITE NILE branch rises in Lake Victoria, south of the Equator. It flows for some 4,000 miles (6,500 kilometres) to reach the Mediterranean Sea through its many streamed DELTA. The Nile has always been the spine and lifeline of Egypt, the great common possession of the two lands. Its fertile valley, varying in width from 12 to 31 miles (19 to 50 kilometres), was renewed each year by the INUNDATION, which prevented the soil from being worked out and enabled a continuity of human occupation. It was the chief means of communication, with a complex network of CANALS leading from it to important towns and temples. Strangely perhaps, considering its overwhelming importance in their lives, the Egyptians never saw the river itself as a god, and the river deity HAAPI is a relatively minor figure in their pantheon. They never discovered the source of the river. The name Nile is first found in the writings of the Greek Hesiod; its derivation is obscure. The Egyptians called it *itr-da*, 'the great river', or even referred to it as the sea. *See also* LOWER EGYPT.

Nine Bows

In Egyptian ART, the PHARAOH is sometimes depicted with his foot placed upon the Nine Bows, which represent the peoples subject to his rule. These included the Egyptians themselves as well as neighbouring peoples like the Libyans and Nubians.

Nineteenth Dynasty

The second dynasty (1295–1188 BC) in the NEW KINGDOM. The first king was RAMESES I (ruled 1295–1294 BC), already an elderly man when he assumed the kingship. He was probably of HYKSOS descent and was succeeded after two years by his son, SETHOS I (ruled 1294–1279 BC). Early in his reign he was challenged by a powerful alliance of Amorites and Aramaeans with the prince of Hamath. He sent three separate armies, those of RA, AMUN and SETH, and defeated all three opponents before they could combine. Like other warrior kings, Sethos was also a prolific builder. The Temple of OSIRIS at ABYDOS dates from his reign, and he continued the building at KARNAK that his father had started. His tomb is in the VALLEY OF THE KINGS. His son, RAMESES II (ruled 1279–1212 BC), was called 'the great' by early Egyptologists, on account of his monuments rather than his performance as a ruler, although both were formidable. He completed the great HYPOSTYLE HALL at Karnak, had temples built in the SUDAN, set up many buildings in THEBES and also rebuilt the city of TANIS, from where his family had originated. Reputedly, Rameses II fathered over 50 daughters and 100 sons. In his reign there was direct confrontation with the HITTITE empire, which hitherto had encouraged buffer states to attack, or revolt against, Egypt. There was a long and hard battle at Kadesh, beyond the Orontes River, in which the Egyptians fought back bravely after a surprise attack and which ended in a stalemate. Rameses's temple walls proclaim it as a major victory, won by the king himself after rallying his broken and disheartened troops. Sporadic warfare continued, with Rameses managing to hold his boundaries. At this time, the power of Assyria was growing, and the kingdom of MITANNI was swallowed up by the rulers of Nineveh. In the face of this threat to both their kingdoms, Egypt and the Hittites made a peace treaty, the earliest of which a written record exists. This was to last for almost 50 years, and the Hittite king paid a state visit to Egypt, bringing his daughter to be Rameses's bride. Rameses died, reputedly aged 100 years, and his son, Mineptah (ruled 1212–1202 BC), faced a rapidly deteriorating international situation. To the east and north the old order was crumbling. There were revolts in Palestine, which he put down. The Hittites were in dire trouble, and he sent them a supply of corn. From the west came the double threat of the ever-hostile Libyans, and the PEOPLE OF THE SEA. They invaded Egypt and attacked MEMPHIS, but Mineptah drove them back. Already an old man, he died after a short reign, leaving a complicated succession problem brought about by the prolific number of cadet branches of the Ramessid royal house. With no clear or undisputed successor, there was a series of usurpations and short reigns during some 12 years, and the state fell into some disarray. For a time the land was ruled by a queen, TWOSRE (*c.*1196–1188 BC), during the minority and again after the death of, her son, Siptah. Contemporary with Twosre was a CHANCELLOR, Iarsu, of Syrian origin, said to have been her lover and accused by a PAPYRUS of the time as plundering the treasury.

Ninth and Tenth Dynasties

Dynasties (2160–*c.*2140 BC) in the FIRST INTERMEDIATE PERIOD. Following the strife-torn EIGHTH DYNASTY, the emergence of the Ninth saw a new power appear. This was the Herakleopolitan dynasty, whose first king was the NOMARCH Kheti I, who seized control of the MEMPHIS kingdom and defeated the forces of UPPER EGYPT at KOPTOS, establishing a somewhat fragile unity maintained by his own ARMY and energy. HERAKLEOPOLIS also provided the Tenth Dynasty, effectively a continuation of the Ninth, with Kheti II as king. The Herakleopolitans cleared the Asiatic invaders from the DELTA, but during the reign of Kheti II the parallel ELEVENTH DYNASTY emerged in THEBES. The Herakleopolitan army invaded Theban territory and captured ABYDOS but was unable to stamp out the rival house. Fighting between the two continued indecisively over a period of about a century.

Nitocris

The first example in Egyptian history of a female king, i.e. a ruling queen. She is shown on MANETHO's list and in the TURIN CANON as a king. There is no archaeological evidence of her reign, which is said to have been at the end of the SIXTH DYNASTY, around 2200 BC, a time of confusion and upheaval.

nomarch

The governor of a NOME, or province, a leader of a provincial aristocracy, with power as administrator, judge and high priest of the nome's own local deity. In the tightly centralized days of the OLD KINGDOM, nomarchs were royal appointees, but from the SIXTH DYNASTY onwards they became increasingly independent and hereditary. They absorbed an ever greater share of the nome's wealth and constructed tombs for themselves on a splendid scale. Their rivalry and refusal to respond to the demands of the central government contributed to the later weakness and eventual decline into chaos of the OLD KINGDOM. During the FIRST INTERMEDIATE PERIOD, there was rivalry and warfare between nomarchs and super-nomarchs who had gained power over their neighbours. With the establishment of the MIDDLE KINGDOM, the role of the nomarchs was systematically reduced, there was a return to central control, and greater rights were granted to peasants and craftsmen, reducing the petty despotism of the nomarch. The last contribution of the nomarchs was to break the rule of the HYKSOS invaders and to bring about the NEW KINGDOM, but with the re-establishment of Egyptian rule, the nomarchs again lost independent power, although the office and title remained up to the end of the dynastic era.

nome

The two Egypts were subdivided into 42 provinces, or nomes, based at least in part on the territories of the tribes who had inhabited the DELTA and NILE Valley in PRE-DYNASTIC times. To this can be traced the continuation of the nome's own local deity, with a god or fetish set up in the temple of the main town, which attracted the loyalty of the inhabitants and at the same time bound it into the greater national COSMOLOGY. The nome was identified by its emblematic god, as in the Elephant Nome (capital Abu, now ELEPHANTINE), the Wolf Nome (This), the Hare Nome (HERMOPOLIS MAGNA) the Two Arrows Nome (SAIS, with its hunter-goddess NEITH). Loyalty to the nome and its god was always strong, and cities such as HERAKLEOPOLIS, TANIS and Sais profited greatly from the elevation of their local lords into the founders of dynasties.

nomen

One of the five names in a king's formal set of titles. The nomen is the king's birth name and is the second in the sequence. It was normally accompanied by the designation 'son of Ra'. This is the name that Egyptologists use to identify PHARAOHS, and it is modern Egyptology that has added the sequential number (e.g. Tuthmosis II) to designate a particular king.

nsw-bty name *see* PRE-NOMEN.

Nubia

The country south of the first NILE cataract, south of present-day ASWAN, known to the Egyptians as Kush. Important as a source of building stone and timber and precious metals. In OLD KINGDOM times it was incorporated as part of the Egyptian kingdom,

Nubian Dynasty

and in the NEW KINGDOM a VICEROY was appointed to rule it, but in the disturbed period of the TWENTY-SECOND to the TWENTY-FOURTH Dynasties it became a separate kingdom and its rulers achieved a reverse takeover of rule in Egypt, between 722–663 BC, the short-lived and unstable Nubian or Kushite Empire. The capital of Nubia was NAPATA, seat at various times of an Egyptian viceroy, of the exiled Theban priests of AMUN-RA and of an imperial PHARAOH.

Nubian Dynasty *see* TWENTY-FIFTH DYNASTY.

Nun

The pre-Creation, a primordial shapeless ocean out of which the sun-god RA emerged. *See* COSMOLOGY.

Nunet

The consort of Nun. *See* COSMOLOGY.

Nut

The sky goddess, paired in the original OGDOAD with the earth-god GEB. Nut came later to be fused with HATHOR.

O

obelisk

A tall monolithic four-sided shaft of stone, usually granite, tapering from base to top and surmounted by a small PYRAMID shape (PYRAMIDION). Originally they formed part of the sun cult at HELIOPOLIS, but became used as part of the processional entrance to temple complexes from MIDDLE KINGDOM times onwards.

ogdoad

A group of eight deities. The most famous is the Hermopolitan, comprising four pairs of male frogs and female snakes, personifying the primeval forces of creation. The term is preserved in the modern town of Asmunein, on the west bank of the NILE opposite AMARNA, the ancient Khmunu or Eight-Town. *See* COSMOLOGY.

Old Kingdom

The greatest epoch of the history of the Egyptian kingdom, *c.* 2658 BC–2185 BC. Its 500-year history spans four dynasties, from the THIRD DYNASTY to the SIXTH. Initially maintaining the pace of development set during the immediately preceding THINITE PERIOD, there was rapid development in many walks of life during the Third Dynasty. For many commentators, the Third Dynasty, that of the first PYRAMID builders, represents a high point of culture and achievement that was never attained again. Up to that point, Egypt had shown an inventiveness, an energy and a technical development that brought many advances of civilization into being. From the FOURTH DYNASTY onwards, a reaction set in. It was as if, to many Egyptians, a pinnacle had been reached that simply needed to be maintained. Stasis was everything. The years, the INUNDATIONS, the crops, would repeat themselves as a regular pattern, and human life and human activity, in an equally regular and predictable pattern, would fit together with the natural process in a divine harmony. The scale and quality of the early PYRAMIDS presented an unanswerable challenge. In the MIDDLE and the NEW KINGDOMS there were periods of comparable lustre and greater international renown, but the OLD KINGDOM was always the yardstick for comparison. Particularly for a people so passionately concerned with tradition and with the past, the shadow of the Old Kingdom and the purity of its rituals and practices during its most brilliant period lay far over the future. When the structures and systems of the Old Kingdom finally collapsed, it was felt to be like the end of the world. It had lasted for so long, had seemed so solid, had left such an enduring imprint upon the soil and the soul of Egypt—how could it perish? After the anarchy, FAMINE and disturbance of the FIRST INTERMEDIATE PERIOD, it was inevitable that the reunified Kingdom should model itself on its mighty predecessor. *See also* FIFTH DYNASTY.

Old Pre-dynastic Period *see* PRE-DYNASTIC PERIOD.

onomasticon (*plural* **onomastica**)
A categorized list of HIEROGLYPHIC words, listing animals, towns, plants, etc.

Opet Festival
The annual processional journey of AMUN-RA, down-river from THEBES to LUXOR and back again.

oracle

Some of the Egyptian gods had an oracular function, especially in the NEW KINGDOM and LATE PERIOD, when the power of the priests was at its height. This was notably the case with AMUN-RA at his temple in THEBES, where the figure of the deity was capable of movement when articulated by an unseen hand.

ornamentation

Aristocratic Egyptians of both sexes had time, opportunity and a definite taste for personal ornamentation. Women gilded their breasts, painted their nipples blue, curled their hair, plucked hair away from places where it was considered unsightly, shadowed their eyes with kohl and painted their palms and feet with henna. They wore anklets, earrings, necklaces and broad-neck collars, bracelets and SCARAB charms. The broad collar, made of rows of differently coloured and sized beads, arranged in a variety of patterns, was the main ornamentation. Throughout the dynastic period, both sexes wore wigs, sometimes with a little conical vessel set on top of the elaborate headdress, which slowly dripped a pleasant-smelling oil down on to the wearer's head. SILVER, GOLD, ivory and precious stones were worn by aristocrats, but shells and clay beads were available to everyone. Dancers wore bead girdles that clicked and rattled as they moved. Much ornamentation was of a prophylactic type, charms worn to ward off specific evils or diseases, or to venerate a particular deity. Other ornaments denoted status, like the scarab seal rings worn on the third finger of the left hand by senior officials or the earrings awarded by the PHARAOH to long-serving courtiers. Earrings were worn by men and women TUTANKHAMUN had pierced ears, although no earrings in place. There were also FAIENCE earplugs, designed to fit into the lobes of the

Osirian Mysteries

ears. Tattooing was common among female acrobats, dancers and prostitutes, whose work required partial or complete nudity. Often they featured the squat god Bes, a powerful fertility charm. *See also* COSMETICS; COSTUME.

Osirian Mysteries

These rites were celebrated at the temple of OSIRIS at ABYDOS but also in other places. HERODOTUS records witnessing them at SAIS. The temples of other gods often had an Osirian chapel attached, for the festival of Osiris, which was a re-enactment of the god's death, burial and resurrection. A number of books have been found containing details of the ritual, including the *Book of the Wrapping of the Mummy* and the *Book of the Opening of the Mouth and Eyes for the Statue in the Golden Building*. A STELE from Abydos, set up in the reign of the TWELFTH DYNASTY king Sesostris III by the Chief of the Secrets of the Divine Sayings, records a royal command 'My Majesty has ordered that you should be taken up to Abydos in the NOME of Ta-ur, to make a monument to my father, Osiris Khyent-Amenti, to adorn every sanctuary with electrum, which he has permitted my Majesty to bring from Nubia, as conqueror and a Justified One.' This text goes on to record the stages of the Mysteries, including a struggle to rescue the dead Osiris from evil spirits, the procession led by Anubis and THOTH to Osiris's tomb, the vengeance and the ultimate triumph of Horus. It is clear that these rites were performed by the very highest officials under the king.

Osiris

The most popularly worshipped of all the Egyptian gods, closely identified with the fertile 'black land' of the NILE Valley. The cycle of his life and death, and rebirth, corresponded to the annual cycle of flooding and new growth in the valley. Among his many attributes was to be the god of the dead, and he was believed to have been the first to undergo the process of MUMMIFICATION before his resurrection. Before admission to the UNDERWORLD, the dead were judged at the court of Osiris. Unlike such deities as PTAH or AMUN-RA, who were essentially gods of the ruling class, Osiris lived within the heart and soul of the people, and his legend is one of the great fundamental tales of Egyptian civilization. He provides the essential link between the far-off sky-gods and the human condition, especially in terms of the AFTERLIFE. References to Osiris are not found in the early dynastic records, and his legend emerges from association with the DELTA god Andzti at BUSIRIS and a later assimilation with Khentiamentiu, god of the NECROPOLIS at ABYDOS, during the course of the FIFTH DYNASTY. The cults of such gods as HORUS, ISIS and ANUBIS were all originally independent of Osiris and appear to have preceded, and been absorbed by, him.

There are four key elements in the Osiris legend—his life, his death, his rebirth and his transfer of power to his son Horus. Osiris, first king of Egypt, taught his people many arts and sciences, including AGRICULTURE, and so gave the Egyptians their staple fare of bread, BEER and wine. He also gave them laws and taught them to honour the gods. His wife and queen was the sorceress Isis. THOTH was his VIZIER and brought the ART of writing. Anubis and WEPWAWET attended Osiris on his journeys of conquest across the world. Osiris was treacherously murdered by his brother, SETH. Seth produced a splendid casket at court and offered it to the man who would best fit it. After others had tried, Osiris did, and it was found to fit him perfectly. But Seth and his helpers shut down the lid of the casket, sealed it and sent it floating down the river. Seth then seized the throne of Egypt. But Isis, wife and sister to Osiris, aided by

Osiris

NEPHTHYS, wife and sister to Seth, searched for the dead king, and they found the chest with his corpse inside it, washed up on the seashore at BYBLOS. Isis brought her husband's body to the holy city of BUTO, but Seth discovered it there and hacked it into many pieces. The parts of Osiris's dismembered body were then distributed all over Egypt, but Isis found them all and reconstituted them with the help of Anubis, the jackal-headed god (said in the legend to have been the product of adulterous love between Osiris and Nephthys), who embalmed the dead king's body. In this mummified form, Osiris lived again, although apart from the mortal world, as ruler of the Kingdom of the Dead. Isis then gave birth to Horus, the posthumous son of Osiris, following a magical impregnation, and hid the baby from Seth amidst the marshes of the DELTA, aided by the cow-goddess HATHOR as wet-nurse. Horus eventually grew up to claim his inheritance and, after a long struggle against Seth, defeated him in battle. In the violence, Seth plucked out one of Horus's eyes and Horus tore off Seth's genitals. Seth appealed to the gods, claiming Horus to be illegitimate, but Horus's claim was found to be valid by a divine council presided over by GEB, and he became king of Egypt.

Thus it was that Osiris and Horus were ancestors of all the PHARAOHS, endowing them with godlike qualities. It can be seen how the Horus of the Osiris legend, Horus the Child, is different from the old sky-god of LETOPOLIS. Osiris himself, with his original fetish object a tree, is in his beginning an agricultural god. The time of his death was the time when the full NILE began to sink. His legend appears in the PYRAMID TEXTS, but its source is unknown. It was brought to the Delta region from elsewhere, and Osiris absorbed the older Delta cult of Andzti, 'the protector', at Busiris. His prestige spread through the two Egypts, he was back-absorbed into the cosmologies, annexed other gods to himself, including Anubis and Wepwawet, and remained the most omnipresent Egyptian deity until Egyptian religion itself was extinguished by Christianity.

Although the Osiris legend can be seen as a metaphor of the Egyptian cycle of flood, growing season, harvest, dry season, with the opposition of wet and dry, fertile and desert, and always the humanly vital aspect of regeneration, commentators have also seen the distant reflection of real social events and conditions within the myth. These events are the abandonment of a nomadic life and the settlement of a kingdom whose agriculture was arable rather than pastoral. There are hints of a culture in which the blood feud was a feature. With the change in settlement patterns came a change in marriage customs, with men seeking brides from within the community (endogamy) rather than from outside (exogamy)—hence the sister-wives of the god-kings.

Osorkon *see* TWENTY-FIFTH DYNASTY.

ostracon (*plural* **ostraca**)
A potsherd, or fragment of a pottery, clay or stone vessel, featuring a written or painted symbol or a piece of script.

P

palace

The king had separate residences in LOWER and UPPER EGYPT and progressed regularly between the two. Although imposing mansions, they were made of mud brick and wood rather than stone, with stone decorative features at the entrance, like SPHINXES and OBELISKS, and were less splendid than the funerary sites.

Palermo Stone

A piece of a black stone slab, now in Palermo, Sicily. Where it came from in Egypt is not known. It bears a list of kings from AHA in the FIRST DYNASTY to NEFERIRKARE in the FIFTH, but the list is not complete. Other fragments have appeared since 1877, when the Palermo Stone was bequeathed to the museum there, but their connection with the Palermo Stone and, in some cases, their authenticity is not confirmed.

palette art

Palettes are small flat stone tools used to grind COSMETICS but also produced simply as votive objects and found in large numbers in PRE-DYNASTIC tombs. These are of archaeological importance in the period before written records for tracing the southwards push of cultural trends from the north, suggestive of a political development also going on in which the kingdom of LOWER EGYPT gained supremacy over that of UPPER EGYPT. These palettes, along with contemporary items such as mace heads, show how the Pre-dynastic Egyptians had already developed a very fine, small-scale ART of stone carving, which in the best examples shows an appreciation of the shape of the slate or stone, fitting the design to the form, as well as a delicacy of effect and sharpness of finish that can only have been accomplished by the finest of FLINT tools.

papyrology
The science of examining and dating the papyrus rolls on which the ancient Egyptians wrote.

papyrus
Papyrus was always expensive, and its use was normally restricted to important documents. Papyrus paper was made from the plant of the same name, a tall, sedge-like marsh plant. The fresh green stems of the papyrus reed were chopped down and cut into manageable lengths. The outer rind was stripped away, exposing the soft and moist inner pith. The pith was cut out and the long slivers laid crosswise on top of one another on a stone surface. They were then pounded and rolled into long flat sheets, pressed and dried. Papyrus rolls up to 120 feet (36.5 metres) in length have been discovered. *See also* WRITING.

peasantry
The great majority of the Egyptian population. They lived in small huts made out of mud brick or reeds smeared with a muddy paste, whose structure varied little with the centuries. Their possessions were very few. The gulf between this labouring multitude and the small number of upper-class priests and nobles was very great. The social division was at its worst during the first dynasties of

Pedubastis

the OLD KINGDOM, when the PHARAOHS were still extending their
power and dominion against a deeply entrenched tradition of local rule. Joined in their family units, and sometimes outside them
into 'battalions' supervised by foremen, the peasants were bound
to the land in a permanent and hereditary serfdom. During the
period of the INUNDATION, when field work was impossible, they
were used as forced labour in the construction of monumental
ARCHITECTURE. Armies of up to 10,000 toiled at individual sites,
supplying by force of numbers the deficiencies of engineering
science. At the end of the OLD KINGDOM there was revolt, when
the peasantry at last found their lot so intolerable that the inbred
respect for the status quo was forgotten. Reforms followed, and
although the peasants remained without any share in the country's wealth, their social conditions were improved. By the NEW
KINGDOM, SERFDOM was declining and there were little
landholdings worked by single families, trading their flax for
foodstuffs or their grain for cloth. Also, the great religious burden that denied heaven to all but the king and a chosen few had
been lifted. From the end of the OLD KINGDOM it was accepted
that a pleasant AFTERLIFE was open to all. This must have spread a
spiritual relief through the entire nation. In periods of peace and
a 'good NILE' their lives, al;though montonous, were not wretched
or miserable. On the whole, the owners of the land were not cruel
or heartless, and the workload was not so great that social pleasures and enjoyment were impossible. The year had its festivals
and rituals, and it can be said that the Egyptian peasant was more
fortunate than his contemporaries in other parts of the world.

Pedubastis

A local DELTA king during the turbulent period of the Assyrian war, who opposed and was executed by ASSURBANIPAL. The Pedubastis Cycle is a collection of LATE PERIOD writings, in the DEMOTIC script, relating the exploits of the legendary hero Inaros and others against the Assyrians. There was a TWENTY-THIRD-DYNASTY PHARAOH of the same name.

Pelusium

A strategic town in the eastern DELTA region, one of the first to face any invader from Asia, and the location of several sieges and battles in the LATE PERIOD.

People of the Sea

A loose term to cover the Indo-European peoples who migrated through the Middle East and across the Mediterranean during the late 2nd millennium BC. A shifting confederation, constantly seeking land to occupy and practising piracy at sea, they made ferocious efforts to invade Egypt during the late NINETEENTH and early TWENTIETH Dynasties but were repulsed.

Pepy I

An OLD KINGDOM PHARAOH of the SIXTH DYNASTY. His reign was lengthy, suggesting that he acceded when very young. He undertook much building in northern NUBIA, and it was at HIERAKONPOLIS that the fine COPPER statue of him was found (now in the Egyptian Museum, Cairo). It was in his reign that the harem conspiracy referred to in WENI's memoir occurred, and he married again, late on, two sisters of a noble family from ABYDOS, one of whom produced his successor, Merenra.

Pepy II

An OLD KINGDOM PHARAOH of the SIXTH DYNASTY. He is believed to have reigned for longer than any other king of Egypt, and may have attained the age of a hundred. He took a great interest in NUBIA from childhood, writing to the governor of ASWAN, who had brought a pygmy back from an expedition, 'When you arrive at the Residence and this pygmy is with you, live and in good condition, my Majesty will do great things for you'—an unusual note of enthusiasm amidst the platitudinous phrases of official correspondence. The early confidence and prosperity of Pepy II's rule degenerated during the king's old age, and perhaps senility, into the administrative and social decay and upheavals that produced the FIRST INTERMEDIATE PERIOD.

peristyle court
A temple or palace courtyard with a pillared arcade on all four sides.

Petrie, Sir William Flinders
(1853–1942) British Egyptologist, Surveyor of the PYRAMIDS and temples of GIZA, and author of many books on ancient Egypt.

pharaoh
The Egyptian king, also known, among many other honorific titles, as 'the double lord' because of the original two kingdoms. The word is derived from the words *per aa*, meaning 'great house'. This is a typical circumlocution, reflecting the awe in which the king was held, by which the chief inhabitant of the palace became known by the name of the building itself. On accession, the pharaoh received five NAMES, beginning with his HORUS NAME, then his *nbty* names, taken from the tutelary goddesses of the two kingdoms, the vulture goddess Nekhebet of UPPER EGYPT and the cobra goddess BUTO of LOWER EGYPT. His third name was called the GOLDEN HORUS NAME. The fourth name

was his principal name, to be used on official records, and finally his own family name, or his private name prior to assuming the kingship. Names were of prime importance, and this is why tombs and the objects that they contained were so liberally marked with the occupant's name and also why a usurper, or restored king of a legitimate line, might seek to expunge the AFTERLIFE of the king by erasing all mentions of his name (*see* TUTHMOSIS III).

The king lived at the absolute pinnacle of human life, at the point where he was partly a god. Even the most exalted of his subjects would be expected to lie prostrate before him until invited to stand. His role was to intercede with the gods for the welfare of the people, and thus he combined the secular aspects of kingship with the active role of high priest. The communion of pharaoh and the gods was a matter of ritual, of formulaic utterance, of giving offerings, all rich in symbolism and performed with a religious solemnity and a sense of human attunement to the cosmic life force that transcended the often (to modern eyes at least) puerility of the charms and spells that were inscribed and uttered.

Normally but not invariably the eldest son of his father's senior queen, the king-to-be was brought up after infancy in full awareness of his ultimate role. He would be solemnly married whilst still a child to a sister, half-sister or cousin. He would be thoroughly tutored in the subjects that it was felt proper for the king to know, including reading and writing, and always he would be taught the gods, their lives, their natures, their part in his ancestry, their multifarious influence on the life of Egypt, their rule of the AFTERLIFE. One day, he would be the master of the spells and incantations by which these immortal and capricious beings

Pharaoh's Day

could be addressed, placated, thanked and venerated. In his teens he would learn the duties of a soldier, and, in the expansionist periods of the MIDDLE and NEW KINGDOMS, might go on a real campaign or even act as head of an expedition out of Egypt. As crown prince he would have an honoured place in the household, his life less controlled by ceremony than the king's, with opportunities for hunting in the swamps and the desert and still treated as a fellow-mortal. On his accession to the throne, he was and would forever remain separate, invested with the qualities of a god. *See also* KINGSHIP.

Pharaoh's Day

The king's day began at dawn, with the rising of his father-patron, the sun. He was greeted with a song of good omen, ushering in the new day. In the temples, singers and musicians were awakening the gods in just the same way. The king's ablutions, bathing, shaving and massage, were performed by servants, he was dressed in his royal garments and took the first meal of the day. The secular side of his life was conducted in the palace, with his chief SCRIBE, assistant scribes, his VIZIER, his CHANCELLOR, and the HONOURED ONES who made up his council. The king took note of letters and reports, and dictated or himself wrote replies, orders, commissions and declarations. These were rolled, sealed with the great seal and despatched via waiting messengers. Accounts were dealt with, a scribe recording in the *Book of the God* (i.e. the king) items of receipt and outgoing. Problems might be discussed with the councillors, most of whom would be members of his own family, including his heir. For public audience, he sat on his throne before the palace door for the two royal offices of judging and commanding. Wearing the CROWN and holding the symbolic crook and flail, he announced decrees or listened to a herald (some of the oldest court offices were designated as The Mouth, The Tongue, etc) perform the task on his behalf and gave judgement on issues. There was no debate or dissension. Those who wished audience of the king 'nosed' the ground before him and kissed it; a specially favoured individual might be allowed to kiss his feet.

The predominant item in the king's routine was religion. Every day had its special religious significance, marking the feast of a particular god or an episode in the life of a major god. Borne on a palanquin, for gods did not walk in public view, he proceeded to the temple. There he was ritually washed and anointed, and the sanctum itself was purified by incense-burning. Then he opened the seals that closed off the shrine of the god and lay prostrate before it as the hymn of worship was chanted. He purified and anointed the figure, took it in his arms and offered it food. Further purifications and anointings followed; the statue was decorated with ornaments and dressed in symbolic bandages before it was returned to the shrine, the doors were closed and the seals replaced. The king left the sanctuary walking backwards, with the traces of his footsteps being sent away. Details of such ritual varied from day to day and evolved with the passage of the dynasties. Often a SACRIFICE was made, with wild animals like gazelles preferred for the purpose over domesticated ones.

The king did not spend all his time on official duties. There was opportunity for leisure pursuits, including hunting. Palace and temple both possessed singers and dancers, entertainers and magicians to amuse the court. His meals were elaborate and symbolic, preceded by rinsings and anointings. The original determinative sign for a meal is composed of a cone-shaped loaf, a beer pot and a

Philae

round cake. A king's ceremonial meal comprised loaves and cakes, but also as many as ten kinds of meat, many different vegetables and an assortment of drinks, including red and white wine.

Philae

A site on the NILE, just north of ELEPHANTINE, centre of the cult of ISIS. The Philae temples have been resited in modern times on the island of Agilkia because of the building of the ASWAN High Dam.

Piankhy

A PHARAOH of the TWENTY-FIFTH DYNASTY (ruled 747–716 BC). King of NUBIA, he stormed through Egypt with an invasion that took the country by surprise and, having obtained the surrender of UPPER and LOWER EGYPT, returned to his capital, NAPATA, as unexpectedly as he had come. He had been brought up in the tenets of the Egyptian religion and was a devout worshipper of the Egyptian gods. His court and society at Napata set out to follow the example of the Egyptian capital, including the construction of PYRAMIDS and MORTUARY TEMPLES.

Pinodjem I *see* TWENTY-FIRST DYNASTY.

Piramesse

A site in the eastern DELTA, selected as capital by RAMESES II and used until the end of the Ramessid era, about 200 years later. Its monumental buildings were later used as quarries to extend the new capital at nearby TANIS.

plough

The ox-drawn plough, which had a huge impact on AGRICULTURE and on society, appeared in Egypt around the time of the FIRST DYNASTY and at the same time as it appeared in Mesopotamia. Previously, a hand-pushed plough or a digging stick or a copper-bladed hoe had been used. The ox-drawn plough, primitive as it was, was incomparably more efficient. It had the effect of 'freeing' labour from the fields, which was speedily transferred to building projects.

population

In the late PRE-DYNASTIC PERIOD it has been estimated at around 1,000,000. By the THIRD DYNASTY it may have been three times as much or even more. It seems likely that throughout the OLD and MIDDLE KINGDOMS, the population was around 5,000,000, except when there was civil disorder and FAMINE, when it dropped rapidly through a combination of early death and high infant mortality. By Roman times, at least during peace, it had attained some 7,000,000. Life expectancy in Egypt was low. Even for a member of the leisured class, the average life span was around 36 years.

Pre-dynastic Period

Corresponding to the New Stone Age, the era between the Palaeolithic civilization of Egypt (*see* PRE-HISTORY) and the rise of the FIRST Dynasty of kings, approximately from 5500 BC to 3500 BC. This lengthy period saw the gradual but steady development of AGRICULTURE and a settled way of life. The majority of settlements were in the areas of MIDDLE and UPPER EGYPT, although they extend from the apex of the DELTA area as far as the second cataract, at Wadi Halfa. Although writing was invented during the Pre-dynastic Period, its lack of written texts made it initially less accessible or attractive to archaeologists and Egyptologists. It was only in the latter part of the 20th century that it became appreciated as not simply a 'prehistoric' preparation but a period of intense interest and great richness. It is now subdivided into separate phases. The Early Pre-dynastic (6th–5th millennium BC) or Badarian Period (from the Badari site in Upper Egypt) is still Stone Age, although at the highest point of development. Pottery was being made, often of a sophisticated design. Already the development of the tomb as a monument is detectable, the medium of its construction being mud brick, although the corpse was simply wrapped in an animal's hide. The Old Pre-dynastic or Naqadal Period, named after the Naqada site in the centre of the Nile's huge bend north of LUXOR, from about 4500 BC, is traced chiefly by means of its highly developed clay pottery, notably in terracotta statuettes. The third phase, the Middle Pre-dynastic, Naqadal or Gerzean Period, takes its name from later finds at Naqada and the discovery of tombs, pottery items and other artefacts at el-GERZA, near MAIDUM. This shows increasing evidence of an intermingling of styles from north and south. Pottery is decorated not only with representations of birds and animals but with devices that may be the symbols of gods. The tombs were substantial, often containing several chambers. The final phase is the Late Pre-dynastic, blending imperceptibly into the dynastic period. By this time the population had grown considerably and there were substantial communities that were fully aware of one another, exchanged goods and shared a common culture and language. The process of political agglomeration had also begun, with larger and more successful communities drawing neighbouring settlements into their own spheres of influence.

If the development of ancient Egypt is imagined in graph form, then the Pre-dynastic Period would be a long, very shallow curve but beginning to rise much more sharply in the last few hundred years of its two-and-a-half millennia duration. Mobile tribal units with ill-defined frontiers were being replaced by agricultural communities organized in larger groups, with enough internal organization to create communal grain stores, manage the division of land after the INUNDATION and engage in mutual and even foreign trade. In time, the tribal units, whilst maintaining much of their own identities and local loyalties, were drawn into two kingdoms. These corresponded to the DELTA area and to the NILE Valley stretching southward from it. The concept of duality, deeply rooted in the ancient Egyptians' minds and ideas, can be at least partly ascribed to this early division.

prehistory

The human race appears to have originated on the African continent, where its most ancient remains have been found. A million years ago the geographical configuration of the landscape and the climatic conditions were very different from now and, indeed, very different from those of the historical period of ancient Egypt. There was greater rainfall in the area, and the Sahara depression was a vast lake. The course and size of the NILE were different, following a course well to the west of the present stream. There is evidence of pre-human habitation in the area of ABU SIMBEL from around 700,000 years ago, and *homo sapiens* has been in the region for at least 100,000 years, as is shown by archaeological evidence from the depressions in the Eastern Desert which once held lakes. A number of cultural phases have been identified, some suggesting regression as well as progress. The peoples of the region had to adapt to climatic change, however slow, as the Sahara assumed its desert aspect and the Nile assumed its present form. The dwellers in the regions that are now arid moved towards the Nile Valley, maintaining a combined riverine and savannah hunting style, living in separate groups. AGRICULTURE was practised at a very early stage, and the use of stone implements displayed skills and tools akin to those of the NEOLITHIC PERIOD. Around the middle of the 6th millennium BC, the practice of AGRICULTURE took firm

pre-nomen

hold and with it settled communities and a way of life that was dependent on the natural cycle of sowing, tilling and reaping, with all the skills that these activities require.

pre-nomen

One of the five names making up the king's formal title. Written inside a CARTOUCHE, it is also known as the *nsw-bty* name, from the accompanying phrase meaning 'He of the SEDGE and the BEE', or *neb tawy* name 'Lord of the Two Lands', both expressing the dual kingship.

priest

Every priest, from the grandest to the most rustic craftsman-attendant of a minor tomb, was merely a deputy of the chief priest, the PHARAOH. They were the keepers of ritual, they knew the formulae appropriate to their own rank and department, but they did not partake of the pharaoh's unique and indivisible power. The Egyptian term for the priesthood was the 'pure ones'. There were two major divisions, with a superior group known as Prophets and an inferior group of Ordinary priests. Reflecting the structure of the court, there was a distinct hierarchy within the temple, with many gradations between the neophyte and the chief prophet. Whilst the priest was of course aware of and respectful to the entire pantheon of gods and their complex and changing interrelations, he was nevertheless especially a priest of the god to whom his temple was dedicated and served his rite in particular. As the year passed, each major and local deity had its own time of festival.

The status of priests varied according to the prestige of their god, their proximity to the court, their birth and their ability. Many of the priests in MORTUARY TEMPLES were part-timers, who were also craftsmen who kept the site in good repair. These men would provide the regular offerings but would command few of the secrets relating to the AFTERLIFE which were the source of the priesthood's vast prestige. But the priesthood, in charge of education and of the magic art of reading and writing, had great power and influence over the secular life of Egypt, although it was a country where the religious and the secular are unusually hard to separate. Doctors, jurists, administrators, architects, could achieve their professional status only through the priesthood. Priests could marry. They had many social privileges, including exemption from the forced labour that was inflicted on most adult males at the time of the INUNDATION. Normally they were free of taxation, as were their temples and tomb cities. Their symbol was a staff of office.

priestess

The priesthood was largely male, with the role of the female priest confined chiefly to ceremonial dance and the provision of music. Allied with this was the role of the sacred prostitutes, found in many temples where the god had a fertility connection but especially those of MIN. *See also* ADORATRICE OF AMUN.

prostitution

In a male-dominated society, where fertility and its display were encouraged, prostitution will flourish. There was nothing furtive or underhand about it in ancient Egypt, where most of the major gods had a strong link with fertility. The prostitute, whether practising under the patronage of the temple or not, had her place in the scheme of things in this cashless society, and there is no suggestion of stigma attaching itself to the profession.

Psammetichus I

A PHARAOH of the TWENTY-SIXTH DYNASTY in the LATE PERIOD. At

Psammetichus II *and* III

this time Egypt was under Assyrian domination, and Psammetichus began his rule by permission of ASSURBANIPAL as a client king. He was king of SAIS, and his rule was at first effective only in LOWER EGYPT. Even here, local lords had considerable independence. He eventually gained control of THEBES, obtaining the surrender of Mentuemhet, who had ruled there as VIZIER of the Nubian kings. Using a composite ARMY of Egyptians and displaced Phoenicians, Syrians and Jews, he gradually established full control. His reign was lengthy, occupying almost half the entire period characterized as the Saite Dynasty in which Egypt once again flourished as a unified state, and a determined, consciously nationalist, effort was made to return to the religious and artistic traditions of earlier times.

Psammetichus II *and* III *see* TWENTY-SIXTH DYNASTY.

Psusennes I *see* TWENTY-FIRST DYNASTY.

Ptah

The local god of MEMPHIS. When Memphis became a royal capital during the FIRST AND SECOND DYNASTIES, Ptah's status grew accordingly. The Memphis priesthood developed a cult of Ptah, which claimed he was the oldest god and had himself created RA-ATUM by pure thought. All other gods and created things were similarly the product of the mind of Ptah. HORUS was claimed to be his heart and THOTH his tongue. The concept of Ptah, although a profound one, was too abstract and abstruse for him to become a true deity of the people. In the course of the OLD KINGDOM, the worship of Ptah, with revivals whenever Memphis was dominant, gradually declined and Ra-Atum became established as the principal god.

Ptahhotep

A hereditary royal official of the Pharaoh WENIS (FIFTH DYNASTY), grandson of a VIZIER of the same name. He is credited with the authorship of a celebrated set of *Maxims*, setting out rules for leading a well-ordered and balanced life. These were much copied during the MIDDLE and NEW KINGDOM periods.

Ptolemaic Period

(304–30 BC) The period that most Egyptologists take to be outside the study of ancient Egypt and more properly part of the study of the Greek and Roman era. But the Ptolemies in their turn assumed the dignities and titles of PHARAOHS, accepted their status as semi-divine and took up such Egyptian traditions as incestuous marriage. They restored many temples and built others. But throughout the country the Greeks formed a kind of upper class, controlling official posts to the exclusion of Egyptians, who resented and despised the Greeks as 'Ionian dogs'. The many immigrant Greeks were contemptuous of Egyptian religion and tradition. During this period the indigenous peasant population, performing their daily tasks as their ancestors had done for thousands of years, were increasingly exploited and impoverished as Greek merchants and magnates took control of production. The Ptolemies could not regenerate Egypt's greatness, as had been done so many times in the past. Egypt was inexorably drawn more and more into the international politics of the Graeco-Roman world, and in 30 BC even the shadow of a kingdom came to an end with the suicide of CLEOPATRA, last of the Ptolemies to reign in Egypt.

Ptolemy

Family name of the last independent rulers of Egypt (304–30 BC).

Punt

A land south of NUBIA, situated inland from the Somali coast, and a

pylon

source of myrrh and other resins and ointments, also GOLD, ivory, ebony and leopard skins. Exploratory visits to Punt were made during the FIFTH and SIXTH DYNASTIES, and the young king PEPY II was very excited by the arrival of a pygmy tribesman, brought back by the governor of ASWAN. Numerous large expeditions were despatched in MIDDLE and NEW KINGDOM times. Such ventures were major undertakings. The route taken was not overland into the interior of the continent but across the Eastern Desert to the Red Sea and by ship to a safe haven on the east coast of tropical Africa. During the LATE PERIOD, the trade eventually died out and Punt lapsed into a place of myth.

pylon
An architectural term referring to a monumental gateway rising above the surrounding construction, formed of two great towers with a gateway between them, all their outer sides sloping inwards, and crowned with a wide, upturned cornice.

pyramid
The pyramid evolved from the MASTABA during the THIRD DYNASTY, as ever more imposing tombs were desired. There was a further reason, which explains the specific shapes adopted for these vast monuments. Pyramid is a Greek word, not Egyptian, possibly derived from a term meaning 'wheat cake', a comestible whose shape may have been pyramidal. The oldest-dated pyramid is the Step Pyramid at Saqqara, dating back to about 2800 BC, and the first great stone monument of the world. It was built as a tomb for the PHARAOH, Djoser, of the Third Dynasty, by his VIZIER, IMHOTEP. Its stepped formation may be seen as a succession of mastabas built on top of one another, and the specific intention, as revealed by the PYRAMID TEXTS, was to assist the

dead ruler's progress skywards by providing him with a gigantic staircase. Secondary reasons can also be provided. As early as this, there would still have been a wish to prevent the depredations of the tomb robber, and also the sheer size and complexity of this structure must have given satisfaction to the great man who commissioned it. At this point in the kingdom's development, the necessary elements of a huge labour force, the raw materials and the constructional skills could all be brought together. The pyramid did not stand alone but was the centrepiece of a group of buildings set around courtyards. The functions of these were to provide a processional route for the KA, or the statue, of the king to promenade, to house priests and to store votary objects, in addition to the MORTUARY TEMPLE and chapels. In one of the latter would be housed the jars holding the preserved entrails of the mummified pharaoh. Just as the living pharaoh moved from room to room within his earthly residences, so his abode in DEATH provided a range of chambers for different rites. His statue in the SERDAB faced two eyeholes in the wall separating it from the mortuary temple, enabling him to see the offerings made to him. A great wall was built around the whole site, itself of ornamental construction and with a single gate. The Step Pyramid itself stands well preserved, but its facing has been lost, and it no longer reflects the gleaming light of the sun as it did when new and for long afterwards. But the architectural details of the interior, and of the whole site, are lively and finely carved and shaped, with a vitality that lightens the massively monumental nature of the construction. The surviving COLUMNS are elegantly slender, with beautifully executed leaf-shaped capitals. The columns take various shapes, some resembling the papyrus stem, some ribbed or fluted, forms that would be reused and adapted many times over in the succeeding millennia. This instant leap into a sophisticated ARCHITECTURE in stone has long been wondered at, but much of its design is owed to imitation of wooden forms. There may have been many more wooden buildings in the PRE-DYNASTIC and THINITE PERIODS than was once thought possible, with their architecture providing inspiration when the use of dressed and carved stone really got under way.

The pyramid of SNOFRU at MAIDUM shows the culmination of the next phase of pyramid-building. Square in plan, it probably began as a mastaba-style construction, with the step formation as at Saqqara, but the steps were filled in with limestone masonry to form a smooth-sided pyramid that reached a peak. Snofru constructed two more pyramids, including the oddly shaped 'bent' or rhomboidal pyramid at Dabshur.

The art of pyramid construction was perfected in the FOURTH DYNASTY with the pyramid of CHEOPS at GIZA, the 'Great Pyramid', a superb feat of engineering, architecture and masonwork. Each side measures 230 metres (754^1/2 feet), to an accuracy of 25 centimetres (10 inches), and the sides are oriented to the points of the compass. It slopes at 51° or 52° and reaches a height of 146.59 metres (481 feet). Its heaviest stone blocks weigh over forty tonnes, and the total number of blocks has been estimated at 2,700,000. Within the structure, entered from the northern face, are chambers, galleries, shafts and air vents, including the 'grand gallery', 48 metres (157^1/2 feet) in length, 5.4 metres (17^3/4 feet) wide and 8.5 metres (27^7/8 feet) high. The method of construction has been long debated, but it seems most likely that temporary earth ramps were built up against the rising structure of the pyramid, enabling the massive blocks of stone to be slowly hauled up and set into position. The work was carried out over a number of years, perhaps as many as twenty for a major work like the Great Pyramid, with a work force of 10,000 or more peasants drafted in during the period of the INUNDATION, accommodated and fed in barracks set up close by—remains of these can still be seen at Giza. The Fourth-Dynasty kings CHEPHREN and MYCERINUS also erected pyramids at Giza, and pyramid construction continued in the FIFTH and SIXTH and subsequent dynasties, several Fifth-Dynasty ones at ABUSIR, the Sixth-Dynasty at Saqqara. But the later pyramids have not survived the storm of time nearly so well as the Great Pyramid; their stone casings have largely gone and they have been subject to erosion by natural and human agencies. From the Fourth Dynasty onwards, pyramids for queens were also constructed, in the vicinity of the king's pyramid and on a smaller scale.

All the pyramids were looted by tomb robbers in ancient times. The Old Dynasty Pyramids were robbed during the FIRST INTERMEDIATE PERIOD, and efforts were made to restore some of them during the MIDDLE KINGDOM. We only know Cheops to be the 'owner' of the Great Pyramid by the fact that his symbol is cut into some of the stone blocks: all trace of his occupancy, the statues, the furnishings, the reliefs, were long gone when western visitors first penetrated its mysterious and awe-inspiring interior. *See also* FUNERARY PRACTICE.

pyramidion

The pyramid-shaped apex of an OBELISK. It represents the BENBEN stone: the rays of the sun caught in stone, set on the primeval mound that rose from the waters.

pyramid texts

Texts engraved on the passage walls of FIFTH- and SIXTH-DY-

pyramid texts

NASTY pyramids at Saqqara, concerned with securing entry into the AFTERLIFE for the deceased. These texts, often repeated from tomb to tomb, are a mixture of PRE-DYNASTIC writings, preserved by tradition, and the later OSIRIS legend, and the conflation of the two gives rise to a certain amount of confusion. The pyramid texts also give an indication of the thinking behind the development of the pyramid itself. The ultimate destination of the dead king was the sky, where he would join the gods. The pyramid, in its original form of the step pyramid, provided him with a staircase (the HIEROGLYPHIC symbol for the step pyramid was also the determinative sign of the verb 'to climb'). In its later smooth-sided form, the pyramid symbolized the sun's rays, petrified—another means by which the king could climb to heaven. The placing of the texts symbolized the two journeys made by the deceased. Those reading inwards to the burial chamber corresponded to the stages by which the corpse was borne to its last resting place. Those reading outwards from the SARCOPHAGUS chamber follow the journey of resurrection, as the king leaves his sarcophagus in its actual and symbolic UNDERWORLDS and attains heaven through his transit of the various chambers and doors, and finally by means of the pyramid itself, reflecting the sun's rays back to their source. *See also* BOOK OF THE DEAD, COFFIN TEXTS.

Q

quarrying

Egypt is rich in stone, and when the development of society in the OLD KINGDOM brought about the rise of stone buildings and a stone-based ARCHITECTURE, quarrying became an important industry. It was necessary to find workable outcrops of good building stone, to quarry it, to cut it into movable blocks and to transport it, sometimes many miles, to the building site. To quarry the stone, slots were first cut into it, then hardwood wedges were driven in and hammered down. The technique of using dry wood and soaking it so that it expanded and forced the stone apart may also have been used. The new-cut block was then shaped with hammers of a harder stone; and copper saws may have been used also, in conjunction with an abrading agent to assist the cutting. Rollers and sledges were used with thick ropes made of fibre to drag the blocks, some of them weighing more than thirty tonnes, into position for further working. The Egyptians were prepared to travel far in search of the right stone for their purposes and knew of deposits far out in the desert areas. Expeditions would be mounted to open up such quarries, following an order from the king or high priest. All this large-scale quarrying activity was carried out without the use of iron tools or of the block and tackle. Time, patience and a huge labour force made up for the deficiency in equipment.

R

Ra *or* Re

The oldest and one of the greatest of the gods, with a complex history of development. He is also known as ATUM, or Ra-Atum. A sky-god identified with the sun, he arose out of NUN, the primeval water, and through his own creation created the elements to sustain life on Earth, with SHU the air-god, NUT the sky-god, GEB the earth-god, Tefnut, the goddess of moisture, NEPHTHYS, OSIRIS and ISIS. The centre of Ra's cult was HELIOPOLIS (Greek: 'sun city') in the DELTA. Ra was perceived in different ways, according to whether the sun was blazing at the zenith or setting in the western sky: this latter was its Atum persona. *See also* AMUN.

Rahotep *see* FIFTEENTH, SIXTEENTH AND SEVENTEENTH DYNASTIES.

Rameses I

The first PHARAOH of the NINETEENTH DYNASTY in the NEW KINGDOM. Like HOREMHEB, his predecessor, he was not of the royal line but had been a general and VIZIER.

Rameses II

A PHARAOH of the NINETEENTH DYNASTY (ruled 1279–1212 BC) in the NEW KINGDOM. Until the sudden 20th-century fame of TUTANKHAMUN, he was the best-known pharaoh to posterity. The early years of his reign were marked by foreign campaigns, culminating in the battle at Kadesh between the Egyptians and the HITTITES. The king recorded this battle in temples at ABYDOS, KARNAK (in three different parts of the temple of AMUN-RA) and at his great temple at ABU SIMBEL, among others, proclaiming the doubtful result as a resounding victory. In the 21st year of his reign he made the first recorded peace treaty between two states, with king Hattusilis of the Hittites. Copies were kept in both capitals, transliterated in the languages of both countries. The treaty did actually inaugurate a lasting peace, and Rameses acquired two Hittite princesses in his collection of wives. He set up his capital at PIRAMESSE, close to AVARIS in the eastern DELTA, a convenient location for his eastern interests—at this time the Egyptian dominions stretched from NUBIA to Syria. In the course of his lengthy reign, RAMESES II built some of the most grandiose of Egyptian monuments. These include the Great and Small Temples at Abu Simbel, the Great Temple being dedicated to the king himself in association with Amun-Ra, PTAH and Ra-Horakhty ('the rising sun') and the Small Temple dedicated to his queen, Nefertari, linked with HATHOR, the RAMESSEUM at Thebes, and many others. Unlike his long-reigning predecessor, PEPY II, Rameses II appears to have been vigorous to the end, and his successor inherited a state that was the major world power.

Rameses III *see* TWENTIETH DYNASTY.

Ramesseum

One of the vast monuments erected by RAMESES II in the NEW KINGDOM period, a palace-cum-MORTUARY TEMPLE on the grandest scale in the centre of the great 'dead city' on the west bank of the NILE at THEBES. Among the elements it retains are a PYLON, HYPOSTYLE HALL, COLOSSAL STATUE and sanctuary. Opinions among

Re

Egyptologists on its style vary from condemnation as outright vulgarity to praise for its purity. The palace consisted of an audience chamber and throne room, with apartments behind. From this a ramp flanked by two colossi led through a pylon to a PERISTYLE COURT, lined on two sides with further colossi. A hypostyle hall led through to the sanctuary area. Subsidiary temples at each side were dedicated to the Theban TRIAD (AMUN, MUT, KHONSU), and to OSIRIS.

Re *see* RA.

Red Crown *see* CROWN; REGALIA.

Red Granary *see* GRANARY; TRADE.

Red House *or* **Red Treasury** *see* CHANCELLOR; TREASURY.

regalia

The prime item in the royal regalia was the CROWN. The White Crown of UPPER EGYPT was a tall, elegant conical hat. The Red Crown of LOWER EGYPT was a flat-topped hat with a high projection at the back and a long forward-curling feather. These two were combined as the Double Crown. In the NEW KINGDOM there was also the Blue Crown, or War Crown, made of blue leather and studded with sequins of GOLD. Around the crown was placed the URAEUS, the ancient cobra symbol of the Lower Kingdom goddess BUTO. Since Buto was also represented as a vulture, and the Upper Kingdom goddess Nekhbet was a vulture-goddess, the uraeus had significance in both lands. In its centre was placed the sun disc. The king's other accoutrements included a crook and a flail, the two instruments signifying his role as guide and shepherd on the one hand (and a reminder of his ancient responsibility for securing the harvest) and as chastiser and source of justice on the other.

Renenutet
A cobra-headed goddess, a protector of households and the harvest. Traces of her worship have been found at Deir el Medina.

Rhind Papyrus *see* FIFTEENTH, SIXTEENTH AND SEVENTEENTH DYNASTIES.

rock tombs
The earliest Egyptian rock tombs are FOURTH DYNASTY, cut in the rock of the GIZA plateau. Their layout was similar to that of the MASTABA, with anteroom, chapel and SERDAB. The tomb chamber was beneath, reached by a shaft from the chapel or from a special antechamber. The entrance, in the rock face, was carved to resemble the structure of a mastaba. The most elaborate rock tombs are in the VALLEY OF THE KINGS.

Rosetta Stone
A milestone in the decipherment of ancient Egyptian texts was the discovery in 1799, by members of Napoleon's expedition, of an inscribed slab of black basalt at Rosetta (now Rashid). A piece of late Egyptian work, it carries the text of a decree of Ptolemy V Epiphanes, in the official Greek but also in DEMOTIC Egyptian and HIEROGLYPHICS. The fragment measures 114 by 72 centimetres ($44^7/8$ by $28^3/8$ inches). The Egyptian text was translated and published by CHAMPOLLION. The Rosetta Stone is in the British Museum in London.

royal marriage
In religious legend OSIRIS had married his sister, ISIS, who gave

birth to HORUS. This sanctified the practice of a future PHARAOH marrying, while still a child, one of his sisters or another close female relation. Later he might take further wives and mistresses, but the Egyptians strongly believed that the pharaoh should have as much royal (and so divine) blood as possible. Kings regularly married their own daughters. Despite this legitimized and holy incest, there seems to have been little of the adverse affects of inbreeding. The extent to which the practice occurred outside the royal family is uncertain, but since it was an effective way of retaining titles and possessions within a family, it may well have been practised by the baronial class.

rubbish mounds

Every Egyptian settlement had rubbish mounds, or communal middens, into which all kinds of waste and debris were pitched. They relied on the heat of the sun, and on scavenging birds and animals to keep the tips from becoming too noisome. Even so, they cannot have been nice to be near. These midden heaps are treasuries for the archaeologist, who can find out an immense amount about people's culture, DIET and living habits from the things they throw away, with the different layers assisting in the dating process.

S

sacrifice

Offerings were routinely presented to the gods and to the dead in their MORTUARY TEMPLES. Meat offerings usually constituted the head, legs, ribs or offal. Wild animals were regarded as superior to domestic animals for sacrificial purposes. It does not seem that animals were slaughtered on a large scale for sacrificial purposes, although FIFTH-DYNASTY SUN TEMPLES have slaughter yards attached, which suggests that there may have been exceptions.

Sahure *see* FIFTH DYNASTY; SHIPS AND SHIPBUILDING.

Sais

A settlement and NOME capital in the eastern DELTA region, centre of the cult of NEITH and the source of two of the later dynasties, the brief TWENTY-FOURTH and the more splendid TWENTY-SIXTH. See also PSAMMETICHUS.

Saite Dynasty *see* TWENTY-SIXTH DYNASTY.

sanitation

In NEW KINGDOM houses of the gentry there is some evidence of small bathrooms and lavatories, but only in larger houses and only adjacent to the master bedroom. The bathroom had a bath place in the corner, a shallow tub of stone in which the bather stood and

Saqqara

had water poured over him by a servant. The water was carefully drained off to the outside or into a collecting vessel; water and mud brick were best kept apart. Lavatories were a luxury furnishing, a stone or wooden seat above a collecting pot that would be taken to the rubbish heap for emptying. Egyptian cities had no drainage. Most people simply used the fields, although houses in towns and villages may also have had trays of earth and sand.

Saqqara

A major funerary site of the OLD KINGDOM, at the southern end of the vast funerary district that extends from GIZA, on the west bank of the NILE, south of Cairo. North Saqqara has the Step Pyramid of Djoser (the first pyramid) and numerous others; among those at south Saqqara are the pyramids of PEPY I and II. Saqqara is rich in other monuments, MORTUARY TEMPLES and MASTABAS

sarcophagus (*plural* sarcophagi)

The chest, made of stone or wood and equipped with a lid, in which the coffin of the mummified corpse was laid. Sarcophagi, especially royal ones, were often extremely elaborate. As the closest thing to the body, apart from the wrappings themselves and the coffin, the spells painted on or incised into the sarcophagus were among the most important and powerful.

Saru *see* LEGAL SYSTEM.

scarab

Close observers of every form of life, the Egyptians developed a special feeling for the humble scarab, a species of dung beetle. This tiny creature was linked to the majestic sun-god. The female lays her eggs in a ball of dung, which she then rolls in front of her through the dust and sand until it is as large as she is. To

the observer, this was the same process as that of RA rolling the
sun's disc across the sky. In addition, the beetle's young emerged
from this ball, in a manner parallel to the god's own creation of
life. The scarab was considered sacred, and millions of representations of it were made, from little lumps of clay to semi-pre-
cious stones like jasper. There were many inlaid pottery scarabs.
All were inscribed with a charm or marked with the CARTOUCHE
of a king or god. The scarab might be pierced to wear round the
neck or was mounted on a ring. Scarabs were inserted between
the linen folds of the mummified corpse.

scribe

WRITING, in its origins, was closely identified with MAGIC, and
the scribe was a respected figure, perhaps even feared on occa-
sion. Eminent men often had themselves sculpted, sitting with
pen, paper and ink palette. Despite the general rule that said a
son should follow his father's occupation, the role of a scribe
was one way in which clever boys from the ranks of the peasantry or unskilled labourers could rise to positions of power and
authority. The scribes' functions were closely linked with the
priesthood, and the apprentice scribe would be a pupil at a priestly
college. Once his training was complete, he would be attached
to the staff of the local NOMARCH or a high priest or, if he were
well connected, the VIZIER himself. As the role of government
expanded, much of the scribes' work was of a secular nature,
making lists, setting out regulations, reporting on the work of
courts or expeditions, compiling the 'wisdom texts' that helped
to regulate social behaviour or reproducing the tale sequences of
Egyptian literature. Such work would be done in the HIERATIC or
DEMOTIC scripts, while the priestly scribe, at a higher level within

the hierarchy, pursued the slower but vastly more prestigious art of HIEROGLYPHIC script. In the same way as 'priest', the term 'scribe' denotes a role that could go far beyond that of writing. Scribes might also be architects, doctors or senior officials of any sort. *See also* EDUCATION.

sculpture

Small-scale decorative stone carving goes far back beyond recorded history. In the PRE-DYNASTIC era, carved palettes were created for ritual and MAGIC purposes. By the time of the SECOND DYNASTY, large-scale stone sculpture was being undertaken, with the first of the superb statues that, with the shape of the PYRAMID, most strongly typify Egyptian ART in modern times. By the FOURTH DYNASTY, contemporary with the construction of the pyramids, sculpture had reached a high point both of achievement and of production. The Egyptians appreciated the plastic possibilities of sculpture, which developed quite differently from painting; it was far more lifelike in appearance. But, like every other department of Egyptian art, sculpture had a function in the scheme of things, and its purpose was religious. The pharaohs and queens who formed its subjects were gods on earth, and even the lesser subjects of their work were attributes or possessions of these same godly figures. If the subject were a lion, for example, although the master sculptor would draw out its lion-like qualities, he would also ensure that its mane resembled the headdress of the king, so that the connection was plain. The sculptor set to work with a definite system in view. His block of stone was a cube, and the cube shape determined the form of his work. Having received his commission, he set about cutting into the cube from the front and sides, leaving the back untouched. Egyptian sculpture was not intended to be seen in the round, and the statue would normally be placed against a wall or column, so that a back view would be impossible. Many sculptures were intended never to be seen by anyone other than the spirit residing in the tomb and the gods. Likewise, many of the finest reliefs were set up in the darkest recesses of temples, where they would never be viewed. To be seen and admired was not part of their purpose. The inscriptions on sculpture were of primary importance to those who commissioned the work: these, rather than the likeness, constituted the identification of the king with the statue and would enable him, when returning in spirit form, to recognize his own earthly image. Later tombs often show evidence of a CARTOUCHE having been erased and a later name added, thereby taking over possession of the figure.

Although sculpture set out to be lifelike, and is often arrestingly so, it did not necessarily attempt to be true to life in the sense of reproducing an actual set of features. The sculptor sought an element of idealization in his work, expressive of the role and status of the figure whom he was portraying. The figures are strong, well shaped, serene, as godlike mortals should be. In the finest examples, their faces and bodies express an immense calm and reposeful dignity. Originally, many of the statues would have been painted to add to the lifelike effect. Eyes were made out of quartz, crystal and copper and carefully inserted in position.

Throughout the millennia, the state of sculpture varied. The Fourth Dynasty was a high point, and later OLD KINGDOM sculpture does not possess that combination of crisp vigour and sedate monumentality that defines the best early Egyptian work. At different times, there are differences between Upper and Lower Kingdom work. Later, there were two distinct phases of development, in the AMARNA PERIOD and the Saite Dynasty (the TWENTY-

Sebek

SIXTH). Amarna tended towards naturalism, sometimes almost extreme, as in a famous sculpture of king AKHENATEN himself (in Cairo Museum) which shows him with the emblems of royalty but a less than heroic physique. During the Saite Dynasty, a determined effort was made to put away foreign influences and return to the sculptural style of the MIDDLE and OLD KINGDOMS. This resulted, not in feeble imitation but in a concern for form, material and expression that produced sculpture of a high order.

Sebek

A deity associated with SETH. CROCODILE-headed, his cult was in the FAIYUM region.

Second Dynasty *see* FIRST AND SECOND DYNASTIES.

Second Intermediate Period

(1675–1553 BC) The MIDDLE KINGDOM dwindled to a confused end, its great glories far in the past, under a succession of undistinguished PHARAOHS of whom little is known, and some writers on Egypt even date the next 'Intermediate' period from the end of the TWELFTH DYNASTY. The peasant population continued to till the soil and maintain the traditional way of life. But the ethnic and political maps were changing, step by step. Already in Egypt there were substantial communities who had come in from the Asian continent, and these increased in size and number as more flowed in, pushed outwards by the pressure of expanding empires, the Hittites in Anatolia, the Hurrians in Mesopotamia (who were ruled by another migrant people, the MITANNI). These peoples possessed skills that the Egyptians had never found it necessary to acquire, including ironwork and the mastery of the horse. They fought from chariots, giving them a speed and mobility that the Egyptian infantry had no way of countering. Gradually, the Asiatic communities coalesced and spread until they constituted an invasion force with its own hierarchy and plans. The process took some fifty years, down to 1675 BC, by which time the invaders had taken control of the kingdom of Egypt. For the first time, the Egyptians found themselves under foreign rule. In fact, the THIRTEENTH Dynasty did not disappear for a further twenty years, but it controlled less and less of the land, becoming less and less consequential, until it simply faded out of history to be followed by a brief, local FOURTEENTH Dynasty (*see* THIRTEENTH AND FOURTEENTH DYNASTIES) based at XOIS, in the DELTA.

The FIFTEENTH and Sixteenth Dynasties were thus foreign ones, founded by one Salitis. They did not impose a foreign system of government and assimilated themselves to the existing Egyptian system. This extended to keeping records in Egyptian script, using Egyptian royal titles and copying Egyptian styles in their art. It indicates, as with the Gothic kingdoms that followed the Roman empire, that the nomadic HYKSOS recognized a superior degree of civilization among the people they had, somewhat surprisingly, conquered. Their kings called themselves 'son of Ra' and they followed a cult of SETH, although they also brought in the worship of the Near Eastern deities Baal and Teshub, who became assimilated with Seth. They also worshipped the moon goddess Astarte. Their first capital was AVARIS, on the Delta shore, then they moved to MEMPHIS. The Egyptian resistance began in THEBES, around 1680 BC, where a branch of the Thirteenth Dynasty arose, founded by Inyotef I, to become the Seventeenth Dynasty (*see* FIFTEENTH, SIXTEENTH AND SEVENTEENTH DYNASTIES), existing simultaneously with the Hyksos Dynasty for almost 100 years before warfare broke out on a large scale under the Theban monarch Seqenenre, who was killed in battle, and his son, Kamose. Kamose had little help from the other NOMARCHS and employed mercenary tribesmen of the MEDJAY. He gained some ground from the Hyksos king Apophis, but it was his successor, AHMOSIS I, who broke the Hyksos, storming first Memphis and then AVARIS. By then the Egyptians had learned the art of chariot warfare.

The Hyksos occupancy had a psychological effect on the Egyptians for two main reasons: they had never been conquered; and they were somewhat shamed by conquest by an opportunistic army of nomadic tribesmen. The imperialism of the NEW KINGDOM can be traced back to this sense of national humiliation.

Second Persian Occupation

(343–333 BC) The double CROWN of Egypt was firmly in the possession of Artaxerxes III Ochos (ruled Egypt 341–338 BC), who had overrun the DELTA with an army of more than a quarter of a million men. There ensued a brutal and vengeful rule, in which the Egyptian population was terrorized and much of the country's wealth, in tomb and temple, TREASURY and GRANARY, was looted and despoiled. Artaxerxes III was followed by Arses (338–336 BC) and by Darius III Codoman (336–332 BC). In the shadow of the Persian rule, in the deep south, perhaps with Nubian support, there is some scanty evidence of an effort to maintain a native dynasty against the day when independence would return, as it had done on so often before. The name of a 'pharaoh' named Khababash is preserved from this time. He appears to have enacted some laws, and a Ptolemaic tradition states that he was fighting the Persians in the Delta in 336/335 BC. But he was not the king in any substantive sense, nor did he found a dynasty. In 334 BC, ALEXANDER THE GREAT finally destroyed the Persian empire at Issus and took

Persepolis. In the following year the Persian satrap surrendered Egypt to the Macedonian who had become Lord of the World.

Sed Festival

A king's jubilee festival, supposedly held to mark thirty years of rule but often held after a much shorter time. The FIRST-DYNASTY king Anedjib celebrated his soon after coming to the throne, probably because he was already an elderly man. The word *sed* means a bull's tail ('mighty bull' was a regular description of a king). There was also a deity called Sed, a dog-headed god who was an associate of WEPWAWET, the 'opener of the ways' to the UNDERWORLD. The festival was a re-enactment of the coronation ritual, with processions to the temples of the principal gods and a lavish production of commemorative objects. Its various rituals were intended to demonstrate the continuing vigour of the king.

sedge

The lily emblem of UPPER EGYPT. The king of the two lands was known, in the allusive style preferred by the Egyptians, as 'He of the sedge and the BEE'.

Sekhmet

The lion-headed goddess of war and sickness, originally associated with MEMPHIS and a figure to be placated.

Semerkhet *see* FIRST AND SECOND DYNASTIES.

Senefru *see* SNOFRU.

Seqenenre *see* FIFTEENTH, SIXTEENTH AND SEVENTEENTH DYNASTIES; SECOND INTERMEDIATE PERIOD.

Serapeum

Among the most imposing of ancient Egypt's monuments, the

serdab

underground galleries at SAQQARA where the sacred APIS bulls were buried, from the EIGHTEENTH DYNASTY onwards. The bulls were the personification of the KA of PTAH, god of MEMPHIS. The name comes from the ground-level temple of Serapis, a composite deity who combined aspects of OSIRIS and APIS in the PTOLEMAIC PERIOD. In the dynastic period, the sacred bulls were worshipped during their lifetime and on their deaths buried in gigantic granite sarcophagi.

serdab

From the Arabic word for cellar, a tomb chamber in which statues of the deceased were placed. It was usually adjacent to the chapel and sometimes eye holes were made in the dividing wall so that the KA could observe the daily offerings.

serfdom

The condition of the bulk of the Egyptian people during the OLD KINGDOM was not unlike medieval serfdom. They laboured as work groups whose selection cut across family ties, and their rights were very few. Following the easing of social conditions after the collapse of the Old Kingdom, matters improved, with families working together and being granted land for their own cultivation.

Sesostris I

A PHARAOH of the MIDDLE KINGDOM, TWELFTH DYNASTY (ruled 1962–1928 BC). An energetic ruler who went farther beyond Egypt's bounds than any predecessor, invading NUBIA as far as the third cataract, acquiring much GOLD and territory. He promoted trading contacts into the Mediterranean and with the land of PUNT, and sponsored many building projects, including a rebuilding of the temple of RA-Atum at HELIOPOLIS. The restored SED FESTIVAL kiosk (the White Chapel) at KARNAK dates back to Sesostris I.

Sesostris II *and* **III** *see* TWELFTH DYNASTY.

Seth

One of the principal gods, murderer of his brother, OSIRIS, identified with the dry desert areas to east and west of the NILE Valley. Seth has sometimes been seen as a Satan figure, but this is not right. In the long-established Egyptian notion of duality, he was necessary, as a counter to OSIRIS, just as the desert was opposed to the valley, and the north to the south, and the dark to the light. The desert had its riches and its charms; and Seth too had his votaries. He was seen as a power who required respect and placation, not at all as the abhorrent entity that Satan was to become. Thunder, storms, whirlwind and hail were all instruments of Seth. The waning of the moon and the occasional lunar and solar eclipses showed that, although defeated by HORUS, he had not lost his powers. He was also a war god. Unlike Horus, his great rival, Seth remained the same unchanging figure in the Egyptian pantheon from beginning to end. He was chiefly identified with UPPER EGYPT, the land of desert, and one tradition had him as the ancestor of the kings of Upper Egypt. As the patron deity of NOMES in both Upper and LOWER EGYPT, he took on a number of animal forms, including that of the hawk but also the dog, CROCODILE, hippopotamus and Oxyrrinchus (the fish that consumed OSIRIS's genitals, the only part of him which ISIS could not retrieve). The oldest centre of SETH's cult is Nubt, on the west bank of the Nile in Upper Egypt, opposite KOPTOS. *See also* COSMOLOGY, GODS.

Sethnakhte *see* TWENTIETH DYNASTY; TWOSRE.

Sethos I

A PHARAOH of the NEW KINGDOM, NINETEENTH DYNASTY (ruled 1294–1279 BC). A military leader and former VIZIER, he rewrote the KING LISTS in order to provide himself with a pharaonic pedigree. It was

Seventeenth Dynasty

he who restored the prestige of Egypt in the Middle East after the neglect of the later EIGHTEENTH-DYNASTY kings, leading successful forays into Palestine and LIBYA, and subduing the Bedouin. His TWO LADIES NAME echoes his success: 'The strong-armed one who renews births and recaptures the NINE BOWS'. His tomb in the VALLEY OF THE KINGS and his MORTUARY TEMPLE at ABYDOS are both well preserved and show ART of a high quality, still very much of the liberated style of the AMARNA PERIOD.

Seventeenth Dynasty *see* FIFTEENTH, SIXTEENTH AND SEVENTEENTH DYNASTIES; SECOND INTERMEDIATE PERIOD.

Seventh Dynasty

In the FIRST INTERMEDIATE PERIOD, from 2200 to around 2160 BC, MANETHO'S text describes the Seventh Dynasty as 'seventy kings in seventy days', a sufficient comment on the turbulence that followed the decline of the SIXTH DYNASTY. A contemporary document known as the *Admonitions*, written by a SCRIBE called Ipuwer, bemoans the disasters of the age and especially the lack of a strong central kingship. A temporary climatic change in eastern Africa at this time, around 2100 BC, caused a succession of low NILES, with a diminution in the crops that eventually led to protests, riots and insurrections by a starving people. Coinciding with the decline of central authority, the stable world of Egypt found itself in a state of imminent collapse, apparently deserted by the gods and deprived of their royal interlocutor. At this time, trading contact with the countries beyond seems to have come to a halt, while Bedouin raided into the DELTA from SINAI and NUBIA relapsed into independent chiefdoms. The successive kings of the Seventh Dynasty (seventeen in six years) were unable to control developments, and it is doubtful how much of Egypt they actually ruled.

Shabaka *and* **Shabitku** *see* TWENTY-FIFTH DYNASTY.

shabti

A small figure in the form of a mummy, made of stone, wood or pottery. They were placed in tombs, and their function was to work for the deceased in the AFTERLIFE, performing necessary tasks like dredging silt from waterways.

shaduf

The ancient Egyptian device for raising water from one level to a higher one by means of a pole set on a pivot, with a leather bucket at one end and a stone counterweight to balance it at the other. Introduced to Egypt by the HYKSOS, it is seen from the EIGHTEENTH DYNASTY onwards.

shendyr kilt *or* skirt

The pleated linen kilt-like garment seen on many representations of kings, with a flat central tab.

Shepseskaf *see* FOURTH DYNASTY.

ships and shipbuilding

The oldest-known pictures of boats come from Egypt. From PRE-DYNASTIC times the Egyptians built boats, out of two basic materials: reeds in LOWER EGYPT and wood in UPPER EGYPT. In the DELTA marshes particularly, boats were a necessity, and from basic rafts made of bundled reeds, the Egyptians evolved more sophisticated vessels capable of seagoing voyages as well as being paddled about the calm waterways of the marshland. Models of reed boats found in OLD-KINGDOM tombs reveal the style of construction, with the reeds bundled together in long cylindrical forms with fibre ropes and extending from a narrow, high prow to a stout waist, then narrowing again to the raised stem. More reed bundles formed the core of the vessel, providing a level deck on which a basket-work deckhouse, on the model of the terrestrial hut, could be set. Most of these boats were propelled by paddles. The mast, on a larger vessel, was formed of two braced poles supported by fibre rigging, and with a broad yardarm to hold a sail in place. Heavy-duty cloth was woven to make sails that could withstand the pressure of wind and the pull of ropes without splitting. Whilst the seagoing capacity of reed vessels has been successfully tested in modern times, it seems more likely that they were used for river and canal work (by far the most common requirement for boats) and that foreign trade was undertaken by wooden craft. The indigenous woods, chiefly sycamore and acacia, do not produce long planks, and Egyptian wooden boats were constructed, without ribs, of short, thick wooden blocks, joined by a combination of pegs and hour-glass-shaped pieces of wood that locked into adjoining pieces. The mast was two-legged, as on the reed vessel; set well forward, it was probably only fitted with a sail when the wind was directly astern. Quite substantial fleets were in existence during the OLD KINGDOM. The Pharaoh SNOFRU (FOURTH DYNASTY) sent 40 ships to BYBLOS to carry back cedar logs. In the FIFTH DYNASTY, Sahure used seagoing warships to harry the Phoenician coast. These ships had no keel and were kept rigid by a stout rope stretched from stern to stern. By then the concept of the rowlock had been developed and ships were rowed rather than paddled. A set of steering oars was fitted at the stern, three on each side. By the ELEVENTH DYNASTY, an official might have at his disposal a whole range of specialized vessels. The tomb of the CHANCELLOR Meketra illustrates his range of river-boats. It includes travelling boats, of different sizes, equipped with a deck-house, kitchen tenders, lightly built yachts with open decks or awnings, a sporting boat and canoe-like fishing vessels. By the NEW KINGDOM, shipbuilding had advanced somewhat. The ships of HATSHEPSUT's expedition to PUNT, which sailed down the Red Sea to the Somali coast, were quite substantial vessels, around 90 feet (27 metres) in length. They had a single mast, stepped amidships on a keel plank that projects forward as a ram. There is no sign of ribbing, but lateral deck beams are in use, assisting stability. Specialization continued. Hatshepsut's tomb shows a substantial barge specially designed for the transport of OBELISKS. It was almost 200 feet (61 metres) long and 70 feet (21 metres) broad, and could support two obelisks with a combined weight of 700 tonnes. To control this mammoth, 27 smaller boats, each manned by 30 oarsmen, were used. One of the obelisks borne by this vessel survives in front of the temple of AMUN-RA at KARNAK. At the other extreme of specialization, the EIGHTEENTH-DYNASTY Pharaoh AMENOPHIS III had a luxury yacht for use on a great ornamental lake within his palace grounds. As with many other aspects of technology, Egyptian shipbuilding made relatively little technical progress and contributed little or nothing to the wider development of the craft.

Shoshenq *see* TWENTY-SECOND AND TWENTY-THIRD DYNASTIES.

Shu
In the COSMOLOGY of HELIOPOLIS, Shu was the air-god (dry), a member of the original OGDOAD, whose partner was Tefnut, goddess of moisture.

silver
Always a rare metal in Egypt, by contrast with the relatively

plentifully available GOLD. As a result, silver was more highly regarded than gold.

Sinai Peninsula

The peninsula to the northeast of Egypt which was strategically important as the land route to the Middle Eastern kingdoms. It was also a source of precious stones, referred to by the Egyptians as 'turquoise land'. It was a desert region, inhabited by roving bands of Bedouin, who were liable to ambush any travellers who were not part of well-armed groups.

Sinuhe

The Story of Sinuhe, dating from the reign of SESOSTRIS I, became one of the most widely copied texts, much used in the schools for SCRIBES during the NEW KINGDOM period. It told the story of the harem official Sinuhe, who ran away from his post in fear at the assassination of Sesostris's father, Anemmenes. He crossed SINAI and eventually reached Syria, where he managed to establish himself as a chief among the Bedouin. But he pined for his own country and regretted his disloyalty. He made application to Sesostris for a pardon, which was granted, and he returned to Egypt to serve the pharaoh faithfully until his death. There was a clear propaganda message in the tale, salted by picaresque detail of Sinuhe's adventures in outlandish places.

Sixteenth Dynasty *see* FIFTEENTH, SIXTEENTH AND SEVENTEENTH DYNASTIES; SECOND INTERMEDIATE PERIOD.

Sixth Dynasty

A dynasty in the OLD KINGDOM, 2322–2151 BC. WENIS, last king of the FIFTH DYNASTY, left no son but was succeeded by the first Sixth-Dynasty king, Teti, who married Wenis' daughter, Iput, and thus acquired legitimacy as king. Teti was an active legislator, and, as his HORUS NAME ('he who pacifies the two lands') indicates, his rule was mainly focused on internal affairs. He appears to have died by assassination, an indication of growing disorder in the state. The next notable reign was that of PEPY I, who was king for at least 40 years, inheriting as a young boy. Pepy worked hard to maintain the unity of the state, with much building in UPPER EGYPT at sites such as ABYDOS, HERAKLEOPOLIS and ELEPHANTINE. Conspiracy within the royal household, centring on the harem, disturbed his reign (*see* WENI). Under Pepy's son Merenra, Egypt carried out invasions into Palestine and Syria and also struggled successfully to retain control of NUBIA against the increasing assertiveness of local chieftains. PEPY II, who followed Merenra, was fascinated by the exotic remoteness of the Upper Nile. His reign was a very long one, between fifty and seventy years, and its momentum steadily decreased, whilst the ambitions of provincial governors grew. It also produced a succession crisis, resulting in two brief and uncertain reigns before the collapse of the Sixth Dynasty and the emergence of the SEVENTH. By the end of Pepy II's reign, the decline can clearly be seen. The court was vast and filled with members of the nobility who enjoyed sinecure positions and who assisted in the intense ceremonial that surrounded the pharaoh. The civil service struggled to maintain the administration, its drills and regulations now centuries old. The principal NOMARCHS, treating their functions as hereditary in a way that would have been impossible in earlier dynasties, were behaving like petty kings, even to the erection of their own NECROPOLISES on a royal scale. The no-man's land of desert around Egypt, although still a protection, was less and less of a deterrent to her increasingly powerful and curious neighbours.

slavery

Native Egyptians were not slaves, however much their condition might resemble slavery. From the late MIDDLE KINGDOM until the end of the dynasties, Egypt had a slave population consisting partly of prisoners of war and partly of purchased slaves. Slaves had few rights in society and were not allowed to practise religion except for the cult of the local fetish. The poorest, who could not afford burial, placed their dead in the river, where the CROCODILES ate them. The better-off slaves had the opportunity to become freedmen, at the discretion of the owner, who was also under a responsibility to ensure that they were housed, fed and clothed.

Smendes *see* TWENTY-FIRST DYNASTY.

Snofru *or* Senefru

A king of the FOURTH DYNASTY (2625–2510 BC). He is the first king, and one of the few from the OLD KINGDOM, of whom some personal characteristics were preserved. He is said to have been a genial and popular figure. Certainly his memory was well preserved, and in the course of the MIDDLE KINGDOM he was deified. In a manner prodigal even among kings of Egypt, Snofru had three successive pyramids built for himself.

Sobekneferu

One of the three certain examples (with HATSHEPSUT and TWOSRE) of a woman who performed the functions of king. She ruled at the end of the TWELFTH DYNASTY, around 1790–1785 BC. Sister and perhaps also wife of the Pharaoh Ammenemes IV, her titles announce her as a woman king. Her rule has been attributed to difficulties over the succession, with no satisfactory male claimant available. Her femaleness does not seem to have been resented, and she is included as a she-king in KING LISTS. Statues of her, recovered in the DELTA area, show her in women's dress, unlike Hatshepsut. Sobekneferu built a PYRAMID at Mazghuna, close to DAHSHUR.

Sothis

Goddess of the star Sirius. The heliacal (before the sunrise) rising of this star was incorporated into the Egyptian CALENDAR

Speos

A temple cut into rock, like those at ABU SIMBEL and BENI-HASAN.

Sphinx

The word may derive from Egyptian *shesep ankh* ('living image'). The most formidable of such statues is the Great Sphinx at GIZA, carved from an outcrop of rock left after quarrying operations and 60 metres (197 feet) in length. It shows the body of a lion with the head of a man, whose headcloth shows him to be a king. It was intended as a guardian figure to the funerary area of the Pharaoh CHEPHREN. There is no evidence that the Sphinx itself was worshipped, although legends and fables were to build up around it, including the Greek myth of Oedipus and the Riddle of the Sphinx.

stele

An engraved slab, set up in a temple or tomb, made of stone, although early wooden examples have also been found. In PRE-DYNASTIC and THINITE tomb sites, the steles might well be the only stone items in constructions of mud brick, their function being to indicate the place where offerings should be made, their text often listing the appropriate items. In later tombs, steles were often employed as 'false doors', imitation doors through which the KA of the deceased could pass in order to find sustenance from the offerings in the mortuary chapel.

stone

The preferred building stone was sandstone or limestone, both of which are relatively easy to cut into clean-edged masonry blocks that fit finely together. Harder rock, like granite, was used for OBELISKS but rarely in buildings, although there is one small granite temple in the vicinity of the SPHINX and the Great Pyramid. The Egyptians explored widely in search of good stone, especially for the fine-grained limestone that would be used for outer surfaces. One of the prime sources for this was TURA in the Mokattam Hills. Hard stone like dolerite was searched out and used for hammers and cutting equipment.

Sudan

The land of NUBIA, or Kush, corresponds to modern Sudan, although the frontier is farther south than in ancient times, when it was at ASWAN.

sun temple

During the period of the FIFTH DYNASTY, and coinciding with the high point of Heliopolitan theology, a new type of temple was built. Compared to the conventional Egyptian temple, which preserved its mysteries in the scented dusk of the inner sanctuary, this was the temple turned inside out. Its holiest place was open to the sky, as befitted a temple dedicated to the sun. The best preserved sun temple is that of King Neuserre at ABU GHUROB. Its nodal point was a representation of the BEN-BEN stone, which was faced by four interlinked altars carved from the same block of ALABASTER. SACRIFICE was an important part of the ritual, and the temple had a stockyard attached, from which the animals were led up to the place of oblation. In other respects the sun temples conformed to the basic temple layout. The sun temple reappears much later, in the NEW KINGDOM, with the rise of the ATEN cult, and the priests of Aten took much interest in the temple forms and worship of Neuserre, Menkauhor and the other Fifth-Dynasty kings. *See also* TEMPLE.

T

Ta'a *see* FIFTEENTH, SIXTEENTH AND SEVENTEENTH DYNASTIES.

Tachos I *see* TWENTY-NINTH AND THIRTIETH DYNASTIES.

Taharqa *see* ASSURBANIPAL; ESARHADDON; TWENTY-FIFTH DYNASTY.

talatat blocks
(from Arabic, meaning 'three hand-widths') the small blocks of sandstone used for rapid building during the AMARNA PERIOD. They were reused on later buildings on other sites.

Tantamini *see* ASSURBANIPAL; THEBES.

Tanis
A settlement and NOME capital in the eastern DELTA region, home town of the Ramessides of the NINETEENTH and TWENTIETH DYNASTIES. Much building was carried out at these times.

Taweret
A goddess with a hippopotamus head, credited with bringing babies to childless women and thus often portrayed on charms and AMULETS.

Tefnakht *see* TWENTY-FIFTH DYNASTY; TWENTY-FOURTH DYNASTY.

Tefnut *see* COSMOLOGY.

tekenu *see* FUNERARY PRACTICE.

temple
The centre of the cult of a particular god or gods. In the OLD and
MIDDLE KINGDOMS, temples in inhabited areas were relatively modest structures, to a scale similar to that of the other buildings. Very
large temples were built on open sites. In the NEW KINGDOM, massive stone temples became a feature of the towns, although they
were by no means open to all the people. It was typical of the
temple to have an imposing doorway; that of AMUN-RA at KARNAK
had 10 sets of PYLON gates, fronting on to an avenue of SPHINXES.
Apart from the gate, the whole temple compound was separated
from the outside world by a high brick wall, sometimes fortified
with towers and crenellations. On festival days, a gorgeous procession would emerge through the gate, priests dressed and decorated in robes and headdresses, bearers carrying the painted and
gilded boats in which the figure of the god rode for its public
progress. This was the only time at which the outside population
had any contact with life inside the temple. The great temples were
important centres of economic life. They owned land, they owned
and jealously guarded mineral rights, their income was substantial, and they were exempt from taxation. They required every kind
of service from the most basic to the most luxurious, and they
provided many other services, like EDUCATION and medicine. The
temple site normally included substantial gardens, with flowers
and shrubs, and also herb gardens, tended for the practical purpose of providing medical and culinary herbs. They had schools
and workshops, cattle pens and grain stores attached.
    The architectural form of temples often appears complicated,
since many temples, of which KARNAK is merely the best-known

example, were added to, rebuilt or restored through successive dynasties, and often with lengthy lapses between building phases. The alterations were often on a totally different scale from the original buildings, as with the sudden growth in the cult of NEITH during the Saite Dynasty (the TWENTY-SIXTH). The New Kingdom temple had a set form. It was surrounded by a high blank wall, so that none of its splendour was seen from outside, apart from the entrance-way. Here there was a PYLON, usually approached from the direction of the Nile by an avenue lined with SPHINXES or lions and terminating in a pair of OBELISKS. The temple was set on an east-west axis, with the pylon positioned centrally in the east-facing wall so that the rising sun shone directly on its towers, dedicated to ISIS and Nephthys. Masts could be fitted into it, supporting banners. Within the gateway was a forecourt, with a pillared arcade surrounding it. Opening on to the court was the HYPOSTYLE HALL, a stately construction of massive columns in rows, creating up to four aisles and lit by clerestory windows cut in the upper walls of the high central nave. This hall gave access, sometimes through a further, smaller hall, to the sanctuary area. As the hierophant proceeded from the bright light of the outside world into the recesses of the temple, the interior of the building became ever darker, more hushed, more full of the odours of incense, more an abode of sacred mysteries. The floor level was raised, to symbolize the primordial mound of earth. Only the priests came this far. The statue of the god was in the NAOS, or sanctuary, with further sanctuaries on either side where other divinities might also reside. (This feature was common in a king's temples, where his own cult would be glorified by association. The temple of Sethos I at ABYDOS had seven sanctuaries.) Such was the essential temple; often they were set on rising ground, where ramps leading from court to court added to the grandeur of the plan. Around it spread an agglomeration of all the auxiliary buildings necessary to preserve the life of the temple and its daily ritual. In the dusk of the interior, the walls were lined with reliefs and paintings, with statues placed against pillars and in niches. Outside the temple, if its grounds were extensive enough, there might be a sacred lake, like the lake of Asheru that partially surrounded the Temple of MUT at Karnak. *See also* ARCHITECTURE, KARNAK, SUN TEMPLE.

Tenth Dynasty *see* HERAKLEOPOLIS; NINTH AND TENTH DYNASTIES.

Teti *see* SIXTH DYNASTY.

textiles

Flax was a major crop, grown in large quantities in designated areas. It was harvested at the same time as the grain crop, and the bundles of stems were forced through large combs in order to remove the bolls. Linseed oil was then extracted from the bolls. The bast fibres were separated by the retting process, steeping the stems in pools, and then spun by use of the simple spindle-whorl into threads of varying fineness. From these, linen was woven on a horizontal loom. Fine linen was highly prized and often stolen, both from houses and tombs.

The Egyptians also produced wool, but it was not used in the tombs. The degree of its use is not known, but it was used for cloaks and shawls for night-time and the cool time of winter.

Theban Dynasty *see* ELEVENTH DYNASTY.

Thebes (modern LUXOR)

In the decline of the OLD KINGDOM, in the period after 2475 BC, Thebes became a capital city, controlling a great area of the

Thebes

NILE Valley and sometimes the entire country. The ELEVENTH and TWELFTH DYNASTIES ruled from here, and presided over many advances in cultural and economic life. As the home of the kings who reinvigorated Egypt at the start of the NEW KINGDOM and after the HYKSOS dominion, and as the cult centre of AMUN-RA, Thebes enjoyed prestige unequalled by any other city in Egypt. It was with the EIGHTEENTH DYNASTY that it became in effect an imperial capital (1580–1350 BC), its domains extending beyond Egypt into Syria. To the whole ancient world it was a place of legend and wonder, for its wealth, its importance and its unique range of buildings. The Nile divided Thebes in two in a typically Egyptian manner, the living city on the east bank, with its royal residence, its government offices, its close-packed houses and the great temple compounds. On the west bank was the city of the dead, the NECROPOLISES and MORTUARY TEMPLES of kings, queens and nobles, spread out as lavishly as the bustling metropolis on the opposite bank. In the AMARNA PERIOD, Thebes lost its role, although not its prestige, until the restoration under HOREMHEB. With the end of the TWENTIETH DYNASTY, Egypt once more was politically divided into Upper and Lower, and in UPPER EGYPT the High Priests of AMUN-RA ruled as kings in effect, and sometimes actually in name, for more than a century. But with the advent of Greek alliances and the threats from Persia and Assyria, the nerve centre of Egypt shifted down-river to MEMPHIS and the DELTA towns. Thebes was left with its temples and its glorious past. When in 664 BC the last Kushite pharaoh, Tantamani, fled back to his home country in the face of the Assyrians under ASSURBANIPAL, Thebes was left open to the invaders, who looted, burned and destroyed the city that had been one of the marvels of the world.

theology

The Egyptians were profoundly aware of their gods, from the local fetish stone to the brilliant, life-giving splendour of RA-Atum and the annual fertilization symbolized by OSIRIS. The GODS existed, but in a non-personal sense. Aloof from the everyday aspects of human life and behaviour, they did not demand or set out a code of moral conduct or supervise the morality of the people. They could be angered and could inflict punishment, but this would be on account of neglect, or an improper ritual, or an insufficient offering. Egyptian RELIGION existed for man to celebrate and safeguard his own place in the universe by worshipping and appeasing the gods; it was not an ethical system. The polarity of good and evil so fundamental in Christianity is not at all present in Egyptian religion, which is based upon the harmony of duality. HORUS and SETH are both necessary, not as crude counter-balances to each other but as part of a more subtly arranged, more fluid harmony, in which good and evil are not extremes and gods may have elements of both. Although gods controlled the AFTERLIFE (OSIRIS as King of the Dead), the next world contained no mutually opposed heaven and hell. Entry to it was not influenced by a person's moral behaviour but by his or her possession of the right information, the magic formulae that were the key. Egyptian religion retained potent elements of primitive magic until its eventual decline and disappearance. *See also* COSMOLOGY, DEATH.

Thinite Period

(3150–2700 BC) The era of the first two dynasties, from the name of the kings' city of origin, This, near ABYDOS. Perhaps the most creative period of Egyptian history, in which the basic tenets that were to govern life for many centuries afterwards were formed or confirmed. *See also* FIRST AND SECOND DYNASTIES.

Third Dynasty

Third Dynasty

(2700–2625 BC) With the Third Dynasty we come to the period of the OLD KINGDOM. This dynasty endured for a period of less than a century and is dominated by the Pharaoh Djoser, or Zoser, and his VIZIER, IMHOTEP. Imhotep, priest and architect, was himself to be deified by admiring later generations. He was the constructor of the first PYRAMID. Despite its massive legacy in stone, the history of the Third Dynasty is obscure.

Third Intermediate Period

(1069–715 BC) Spanning the TWENTY-FIRST to the Twenty-third Dynasties (*see* TWENTY-SECOND AND TWENTY-THIRD DYNASTIES), this era opens the final millennium of ancient Egypt's history and corresponds to the Biblical period of David and Solomon. Apart from a brief time of unified rule by the Theban priest-king Pinudjem I, it was marked by divisions within the kingdom, with pharaohs in control only of LOWER EGYPT and UPPER EGYPT ruled by the hereditary chief priests at THEBES, sometimes as crowned kings. The Theban rule was a theocracy, with AMUN-RA at its head. The statue of the god was turned into an ORACLE and manipulated by the priest to provide appropriate answers. Thebes had no foreign policy, and the pharaohs of Memphis were incapable of firm rule. The international standing of Egypt sank to a low level until the assumption of power by Shoshenq I and the commencement of the Twenty-second, or Libyan, Dynasty. The Libyans ruled for a century and a half, with their base in the north, until a branch set up a separate kingdom at Thebes, the Twenty-third Dynasty, whose succession of five kings co-existed with the parent branch until the uprising of Tefnakht at SAIS, and the invasion of the Nubians, which brought the era to a close.

Thirteenth and Fourteenth Dynasties

(1785–c.1675 BC) These two dynasties in the MIDDLE KINGDOM
are little known, and the KING LISTS of the time are confused and
sometimes contradictory. It was a lengthy period in which no
individual reign stands out among some 25 pharaohs. During
this period, the unity and cohesion of the state were maintained,
although in the later stages there is evidence of social unrest and
the uncertainty of central rule that allowed the more dynamic
immigrant HYKSOS community first to extend its own area of
control in the DELTA and then take over the monarchy of the whole
country, with the imposition of the FIFTEENTH DYNASTY.

Thirtieth Dynasty *see* TWENTY-NINTH AND THIRTIETH DYNASTIES.

This *see* FIRST AND SECOND DYNASTIES; THINITE PERIOD.

Thoth

An early rival to RA, the sun-god, as creator of Egypt (and hence
the world). In the dark before the sun, Thoth summoned the gods
who produced the egg from which the sun hatched. These were
animal gods, four frogs and four snakes, known collectively as
the OGDOAD. Thoth, depicted as a man with the head of an ibis
was the SCRIBE of the gods, the inventor of WRITING, language and
MAGIC. His wife was Seshat, who wrote the details of every human life on the leaves of the Tree of Heaven. There was considerable animosity between the priesthood of Thoth and that of
Ra. The centre of Thoth's cult were the cities of Hermopolis
(Greek: 'city of Hermes'), one in the DELTA, one in MIDDLE EGYPT.

Ti *see* FIFTH DYNASTY.

time

The Egyptians measured the day into twelve hours of light and

twelve of darkness, whatever the real duration of daylight. In the
tropics, the division of light and dark is more constant than farther
north or south. They used sundials to measure the passage of time,
and in the NEW KINGDOM the water clock was developed. However,
a glance at the position of the sun would have been enough to tell
any Egyptian what the time of day was. By night, for religious or
magical purposes, the hour could be told by observing the positions of the stars. *See also* CALENDAR.

Tiy

A notable queen of the NEW KINGDOM, principal wife to the Pharaoh AMENOPHIS III and mother of AKHENATEN (EIGHTEENTH DYNASTY).
She was a commoner, although her father was a court official of
some importance, Master of the Stud Farm.

tomb

From PRE-DYNASTIC times up to the end of the dynastic period, the
vast majority of the population were buried in pits, with a few possessions that could be spared to equip them for the AFTERLIFE. Tombs
were not for them. In the OLD KINGDOM, tombs were for the king
and his closest family and advisers, but by the NEW KINGDOM, people well down the social scale were building tombs (*see* DEIR EL
MEDINA). For the wealthy Egyptian, his tomb was a more important consideration than his dwelling house during his life. It would
reflect his wealth and prestige, and should contain a suitable range
of artefacts in order to maintain these throughout the long, long
future, and above all it would perpetuate his name. It should be
made durable for the same reason. Its position was important, pref-
erably close to the main PYRAMID of the pharaoh or a great man
whom he had served or, failing that, in some particularly sacred
site such as ABYDOS, where, according to legend, the head of OSIRIS

was buried. Pharaohs had more than one tomb, usually having one provided in LOWER and one in UPPER EGYPT. One of these was a cenotaph, or empty tomb, since the mummified body could only be in one place. *See also* ARCHITECTURE, DEATH, MASTABA, PYRAMID.

tomb robbers

The constructors of tombs, particularly PYRAMIDS, sought to make them secure against intruders, with false doors and entrances, decoy corridors and massive portcullis-type barriers, whilst the tomb robbers sought for new ways of getting in to reach the tomb chamber and its adjacent rooms. During times of FAMINE and political unrest, when public order had broken down or was only sporadically imposed, the lure of the riches of the tombs outweighed the ingrained respect for the dead, and tomb robbing became rife. The desperation of the rulers is shown by the EIGHTEENTH DYNASTY's decision to build concealed tombs in the VALLEY OF THE KINGS. During the incompetent reigns of the later TWENTIETH-DYNASTY kings, tomb robbing was practised on such a scale as to scandalize the entire country, and it was clear that often the robbers were workmen who knew exactly where to go and what to look for. As a result of despoliation of the tombs, only one royal tomb, that of TUTANKHAMUN, reached the 20th century AD without being ransacked. There was also a degree of official tomb robbing. Certain kings found it more convenient to annex a tomb rather than to construct one. Statues from older tombs were also removed, their CARTOUCHES obliterated and new ones incised in their place since it was only the name that counted. *See also* CRIME AND PUNISHMENT.

trade

(1) *internal trading* trading is so old a practice that its origins are lost. Ever since human communities began to talk to one an-

other, trade has probably been practised, first of all in the form of ceremonial exchanges, soon followed by bartering. Barter and payment in kind remained the basis of trading within Egypt right up until the time of the Persian conquest. Until the MIDDLE KINGDOM, individual communities tended to be self-sufficient. An estate, whether crown land, under a provincial baron, or attached to a temple or royal tomb, could cater for virtually all its everyday needs. The existence of the two granaries (*see* GRANARY), the Red Granary of the DELTA and the White Granary of UPPER EGYPT, indicates some central provision for the storing of surpluses and for distribution in time of shortages. Property could be acquired, by barter or exchange, and there were set standards to establish the value of transactable items. Profit and loss would seem to be excluded from this system, but many lawsuits reflect the disappointment of buyers who found that the goods for which they had made exchange did not live up to the vendor's description.

(2) *external trading* virtually all Egypt's imports, with the exception of long timber, could be described as luxury goods. The wood came from Lebanon and Syria by sea. There were also land trading routes in that direction, more hazardous because of the hostile Bedouin, and other items coming from or through the Middle Eastern lands include lapis lazuli and wine. Caravan routes linked Egypt, through NUBIA and the lands beyond, with the tropical African regions. Ebony, ivory, hides, exotic beasts, ostrich feathers and GOLD all came that way, or by sea from round the Horn of Africa to a port on the Red Sea coast, and then by a toilsome mule train across the Eastern Desert. The PALERMO STONE records commodities brought from the land of PUNT, including 80,000 measures of myrrh, 6,000 units of ELECTRUM, 2,900 units of wood and 23,020 measures of unguents. The value of these

must have been immense. Much of what came in from the south may have been the result of raids, or simply taking, rather than trade, but in the later centuries some form of exchange was practised about which little is known. Other items came into Egypt in the form of tribute, during the periods of imperial expansion, or as gifts from friendly or anxious neighbours. Much Egyptian GOLD went on the outward journey for the same reason. Actual exports from Egypt reflected the country's capacity for manufacture of luxury goods. They included made-up medicines, fine furniture and pottery, oils, and cloth. *See also* ECONOMY.

transport

The principal artery of travel was the NILE. Many of the CANALS that drew water from the main river were navigable, and for any major building project within a reasonable distance of the stream, it was easiest to construct a canal through the soft earth in order to transport the tonnages of stone and the major timbers required. A wide variety of shipping was developed. Vessels had to cope with the upstream way, against the flow of the river, as well as the easy downstream passage. Movement up and down the river was highly organized. For the benefit of the court, rest houses were built on the riverbanks, with a permanent staff and farmland. *See also* SHIPS AND SHIPBUILDING.

Roads were few and rudimentary. As with canals, a road might be made for a specific purpose and then revert to cultivated fields. Although the wheel was known to the Egyptians, they made no serious use of it, at least until the HYKSOS period, when the war chariot became an important part of military equipment. Wheeled vehicles might have sunk in the lightweight road surfaces, where traditional vehicles spread their weight widely and with an even

treasury

pressure. Hauliers used sleds, often of massive construction, which were pulled by oxen and slid along trackways that had been specially watered so that the runners moved easily along, supported by a thin layer of mud. Freight that could be readily broken up into smaller packages would be carried overland by mule trains. Over shorter distances, many burdens were carried by the peasants themselves, with yokes with leather water buckets, bundles of faggots, baskets of fish and grain. Along and between the irrigation canals and ditches were pathways formed by the regular imprint of human feet and animal hooves.

treasury

The kingdom possessed two great treasuries, the White Treasury of UPPER EGYPT and the Red Treasury of LOWER EGYPT. Under the control of the CHANCELLOR or a deputy, these were repositories of the GOLD and precious metal mined in and around Egypt or brought into the country as a result of trade and tribute. Although there was no CURRENCY, gold by weight was used as a medium of exchange by those who had it. All precious metal was under direct royal control. The gold of Egypt was legendary in the ancient world, and by the NEW KINGDOM, friendly kings did not hesitate to ask for it in gifts, and it was also extensively used to pay the salaries of the vast numbers of mercenary soldiers employed during the LATE PERIOD. *See also* ECONOMY.

triad

A traditional triple grouping of deities, usually father, mother and son (as in AMUN, MUT and KHONSU).

Tura

Much of the best building limestone came from the famous quarries at this site at the apex of the DELTA, on the eastern bank from Saqqara.

Turin Canon

a KING LIST, written on a fragmentary papyrus roll, now preserved in the Egyptian Museum, Turin.

Tutankhamun

This EIGHTEENTH-DYNASTY king (ruled 1336–1327 BC), who died at 18, has enjoyed more fame in recent times than he did when alive. He was an ineffectual ruler, of somewhat obscure origins, his name originally Tutankhaten until the discrediting of the ATEN cult, when the priests of AMUN—the real power in the land—changed it. He was buried in the VALLEY OF THE KINGS, and his tomb survived unviolated until 1922, when it was discovered and opened by Howard CARTER. Its magnificence stunned the world, brought ancient Egypt to public attention and made Egyptologists speculate wistfully on what might have been found in the tomb of a great pharaoh, a Tuthmosis or Sesostris. In the antechamber were found a wide range of objects, gilded and jewelled chairs, stools, model boats, chariots, different sorts of weaponry, chests containing items of clothing, and mummified birds. Two life-size statues of the king stood by the sealed door into the burial chamber. The mummy of the king, its face covered by a superb mask, perhaps the best-known single piece of Egyptian ART, lay within the innermost of three coffins, made of solid GOLD and profusely ornamented with turquoise, lapis lazuli, carnelians and other jewels. The outer coffin, of stone, lay within a series of shrines made of gold. In another chamber were found the chest containing the king's entrails, a large quantity of votive objects and, among other things, an ivory fan, its feathers still perfectly preserved.

Tuthmosis I

A NEW KINGDOM pharaoh of the EIGHTEENTH DYNASTY (ruled 1506–1493 BC). An able soldier who held the frontier of the Egyptian empire against the Mitanni, he also began the transformation of the temple of AMUN-RA at KARNAK. Tuthmosis I inaugurated the practice of royal burial in the VALLEY OF THE KINGS. The definitive version of the BOOK OF WHAT IS IN THE UNDERWORLD was found on the walls of his burial chamber.

Tuthmosis II *see* EIGHTEENTH DYNASTY; HATSHEPSUT.

Tuthmosis III

A NEW KINGDOM pharaoh of the EIGHTEENTH DYNASTY (ruled 1479–1425 BC). One of the great kings of Egypt, who acceded at the age of six but whose career was frustrated at its start by the usurpation of the throne by his redoubtable aunt, Queen HATSHEPSUT, who was acting as regent. Tuthmosis finally regained his position around 1458 BC, and immediately found himself involved in warfare with MITANNI. It took 17 campaigns to make good the boast of his predecessor, TUTHMOSIS I, that Egypt's border was on the Euphrates. Tuthmosis III took his army across the Euphrates on rafts to win victory in the Mesopotamian heartland. The walls of the Temple of AMUN-RA at KARNAK bear the legend of his conquests. He made Egypt the supreme power in the Middle East, and tribute was sent to him from as far away as Adana in present-day Turkey. Tuthmosis tried hard but in vain to obliterate all mentions of the name of Hatshepsut in the many buildings she had erected. His own record as a builder includes further work on the temple of AMUN-RA at KARNAK (the colonnade), as well as at DEIR EL BAHRI and MEDINET HABU. The OBELISKS on the Thames Embankment in London and in Central Park, New York, were originally set up by Tuthmosis III at HELIOPOLIS. He was buried in the VALLEY OF THE KINGS; his mummy has been preserved and shows him to have been a short man, like some other great military leaders.

Tuthmosis IV *see* EIGHTEENTH DYNASTY.

Twelfth Dynasty

(1991–1785 BC) A dynasty in the MIDDLE KINGDOM. The first king was AMMENEMES I, who had been VIZIER to the previous ELEVENTH-DYNASTY king. There were other claimants to the throne, who had to be fought down, and the king, who was the son of a priest named Sesostris, was keen to prove his legitimacy, and had a literary work composed, set in the reign of SNOFRU, to foretell his own reign: 'A king will come from the south. He will take the white crown, he will take the red crown; he will join the two mighty ones'. Ammenemes moved the capital from THEBES to a site in MIDDLE EGYPT, although Thebes, with the temple of AMUN-RA, remained a place of major importance. He introduced a new element into the kingship, which most of his successors were to follow, by bringing his crown prince, SESOSTRIS I, in as co-regent. This enabled the king to go on campaign while having less fear of the same kind of coup that had brought himself to power, and also introduced the heir to the responsibilities of the kingship. In 1962 BC Ammenemes was murdered after a conspiracy in the harem; Sesostris was on campaign in the Libyan desert and presumably not involved. He acceded to the throne and maintained a vigorous rule, finally reconquering LOWER NUBIA and extending fortresses up to the third cataract. His son, Ammenemes II, inherited (1928 BC) and duly passed on a stable and wealthy kingdom, with extensive trading and cultural links into the whole eastern

Twelfth Dynasty

Mediterranean and Near East. Sesostris II (ruled 1895–1878 BC) began a major reclamation work in the FAIYUM, which was not completed until the reign of his grandson, Ammenemes III. Sesostris II set up his own tomb complex in the region, at el-Lahun. Wth prolonged peace and prosperity, the provincial aristocracy again became powerful and threatened the effectiveness of central administration. Sesostris III (ruled 1878–1842 BC) tackled this problem resolutely, reducing the power of the nobles and appointing civil servants under three VIZIERS for LOWER EGYPT, UPPER EGYPT and Lower Nubia. The long reign of Ammenemes III (1842–1797 BC) saw the peak of the MIDDLE KINGDOM. The vast work of transforming the FAIYUM from marsh to crop land was complete, opening up a great tract of land for the expanding population and bringing a vast increase to the national yield. Many foreign workers crowded into Egypt at this time as economic migrants, bringing a large Asiatic element into the population. Such opulence was inevitably translated into stone. Ammenemes III had two colossal granite figures of himself set up on limestone bases at Biahmu and constructed one PYRAMID at DAHSHUR and another at Hawara, beside which are the remains of his MORTUARY TEMPLE. Many other temples and fortifications were constructed at the time.

Despite the great wealth of the land and the peacefulness of the times, decline was setting in. After the short reign of Ammenemes IV (1797–1790 BC), there was a brief period of disputed succession that brought the dynasty to an end. At this time, a queen came to exercise supreme power, SOBKNEFERU ('the beauty of Sobek'), who was Ammenemes' sister and perhaps wife. Her rule was brief and may have ended with her assassination.

Twentieth Dynasty

(1188–1069 BC) A dynasty in the NEW KINGDOM. The first king was Sethnakhte (ruled 1188–1186 BC). In this brief time he reimposed a firm central rule after the collapse of the NINETEENTH DYNASTY. His son, Rameses III (ruled 1186–1154 BC), was another pharaoh of great ability. Internal reforms were made, defining the status and rights of every member of the community. The imperial tribute was exacted from client kings once again, trading expeditions went out, mining was resumed in areas where banditry had made it impossible, and a great building programme was launched. The long process of building the temple at KARNAK continued, and Rameses III also built at Thebes and set up his own great temple at MEDINET-HABU. All this was achieved against a state of almost permanent warfare. The Libyans attacked again and were repulsed again. The PEOPLE OF THE SEA attempted a direct invasion by sea and land, and a great sea battle was fought off the DELTA, with archers firing from the ships and the vessels then ramming the enemy. Fought off, the invaders returned four years later and were again heavily defeated. A period of peace ensued, but Rameses III's reign was troubled by a plot, which originated in the harem but appears to have involved numerous officials, to manipulate the succession. The affair was discovered, and the chief plotters, including the king's son, compelled to commit suicide; others had their ears and noses slit. The Twentieth Dynasty continued under a further eight Rameses in a state of steady decline. The priesthood of AMUN-RA, whose temple had received much of Rameses' plunder, was the main power in the state, but its attention was focused on its own cult and the preservation of its oligarchic status, without concern for civil order. With a lack of firm central government, civil unrest grew.

Twenty-eighth Dynasty

Food supplies were inefficiently distributed, and there was a situation similar, although less drastic, to that so deplored by Ipu-wer in his admonitions during the FIRST INTERMEDIATE PERIOD.

Twenty-eighth Dynasty

(404–399 BC) A dynasty in the LATE PERIOD that consisted of the reign of a single king, Amyrtaeus, a lord of SAIS in the DELTA, who drove out the residual Persian garrison in 404 BC. Little is known about his actual reign.

Twenty-fifth Dynasty

(747–656 BC) A dynasty in the LATE PERIOD, also known as the Nubian Dynasty. Under the Libyan kings, NUBIA had ceased to be an Egyptian possession or dependency, but it retained some of the character of a colony. During the EIGHTEENTH DYNASTY, a viceroyalty had been set up in Nubia, centred on the city of NAPATA, and its court had reproduced all the main features of the royal court of THEBES. The cult of AMUN-RA was celebrated there and took a strong hold on the Nubian population. When the priest-kings of Thebes were supplanted by the Libyan Dynasty, many of the priesthood took refuge in Nubia. The temple at Napata became a sort of Thebes in exile, and the cult was carried on even when Nubia slipped entirely out of the control of the rulers of Egypt. For two centuries of Libyan domination the tradition was maintained. Egyptian was the official language of government, and in some ways, as Egypt appeared to have lost its imperial pride, the Nubians prided themselves on being more Egyptian than the Egyptians.

In a surprise move, their king, PIANKHY, launched an invasion of Egypt from the south, transporting his army down the NILE in a huge flotilla of boats. They encountered Tefnakht, the local prince or governor of SAIS, at Thebes and defeated him there, then fought their way on down-river, taking Hermopolis, MEMPHIS and finally overrunning the DELTA. The Egyptians made submission to Piankhy, and Tefnakht on his surrender was treated honourably by the Nubian king. Then, his conquest complete, Piankhy and his army abandoned Egypt and returned up the Nile to their distant capital. No attempt was made to leave an administration. The last king of the Libyan Dynasty, Osorkon, reoccupied Thebes and set up his own rule again. Tefnakht resumed his control of Memphis and the Delta (*see* TWENTY-FOURTH DYNASTY). Piankhy's motives for invasion remain obscure. He may have been prompted by an ORACLE of Amun-Ra, transmitted through the priests, anxious to return to their ancient sanctuary at Thebes. It does not appear to have been for gain or for empire. But the Nubians had not finished with Egypt. Piankhy's son and successor, Shabaka (ruled 716–702 BC), invaded Egypt, brought the Libyan Dynasty and the Twenty-fourth Dynasty to an end, and set up his capital at Thebes. He shared the piety of his father despite his reputation for cruelty, as with the death of Bocchoris (*see* TWENTY-FOURTH DYNASTY). During his reign temples were renovated throughout the country. He treated with the Assyrians, avoiding war on that front. His successor was Shabitku (ruled 702–690 BC), during whose reign confrontation with Assyria could not be avoided, and an alliance was made with the kingdom of Judah. His uncle, Taharqa, led an army into Palestine, where Sennacherib, king of Assyria, was besieging Jerusalem. At this time the Assyrians were struck by the mysterious plague described in the Biblical Book of Kings, and war was again delayed. In 690 BC, Taharqa had Shabitku murdered and assumed the throne himself. He moved his capital to TANIS, in the eastern Delta, from which forward position he hoped to mount an empire-building campaign into the Near East. Taharqa was an efficient administrator and planner. Military governors were installed at Thebes and Napata, and the priests of Amun-Ra were forbidden to participate in civil affairs. In 671 BC the Assyrian King ESARHADDON finally launched a direct attack on Egypt. Whilst Taharqa awaited him in the Delta, the Assyrian marched directly on Memphis, capturing the city and cutting the Egyptians' lines of communication. Taharqa's family was captured by the Assyrians and the pharaoh himself fled back to Nubia. His governor at Thebes duly surrendered to Esarhaddon. Esarhaddon, by now overlord of a vast extent of the Middle East, did not remain in Egypt. He left a garrison and obtained the dubious allegiance of many Egyptian lords, especially those of the Delta. On the Assyrian king's departure, Taharqa returned and retook Memphis. His possession was only for a few years before Esarhaddon's successor, ASSURBANIPAL, came with a vast force and captured Memphis and Thebes. Taharqa died in 664 BC and was followed by Tantamani (ruled 664–656 BC). He invaded Egypt from Napata in order to drive out the Assyrians, but Assurbanipal forced him back into Nubia. The Nubian Dynasty was at an end. The kings retreated deep into their vast country, setting up a new capital at Meroe, between the fifth and sixth cataracts. Gradually the land of Kush was to acquire a mythic status for the Egyptians.

Twenty-first Dynasty

(1069–945 BC) A dynasty in the THIRD INTERMEDIATE PERIOD. The result of the feeble rule of the last Ramessids was a lapse into the division of the two lands. The first king was Smendes (ruled 1069–1043 BC), a VIZIER of LOWER EGYPT, who set up his capital in the DELTA city of TANIS. UPPER EGYPT was ruled from THEBES, where HERIHOR, who combined the offices of high priest of AMUN and vizier of UPPER EGYPT, was installed as effective king. Unity was briefly restored when his grandson, Pinodjem I, who at first had 'reigned' as high priest, formally assumed the kingship and ruled at Tanis (1054–1042 BC). But Tanis was an outstation of Thebes rather than a Delta power at that point. In the reign of Pinodjem I the royal mummies that had been violated and robbed in the VALLEY OF THE KINGS were rewrapped and reinterred in a secret place behind the temple of Hatshepsut, where they were found in modern times. After his death, power fluctuated between Tanis and Thebes; sometimes, as with Psusennes I (ruled 1039–993 BC), under a single king, more often under a combination of king in the north and high priest in the south, operating in uneasy coalition. The strings were generally pulled from Thebes, despite the royal status of Tanis. The priests were the real rulers, using the oracular powers of Amun-Ra to deal with all questions.

Twenty-fourth Dynasty

(727–715 BC) A brief dynasty of two kings in the THIRD INTERMEDIATE PERIOD. Its founder was Tefnakht, the local prince or governor of the DELTA city of SAIS, who made himself master of the Delta, taking BUBASTIS and TANIS, and then moved on UPPER EGYPT, capturing Hermopolis and MEMPHIS, and laying siege to Herakleopolis, when the Nubian invasion brought his venture to a sudden halt (*see* TWENTY-FIFTH DY-

NASTY). On the departure of the Nubians, he regained control of LOWER EGYPT and was succeeded by his son, Bocchoris, who ruled well, playing a careful diplomatic game with the Assyrians under Sargon II. He was favourably remembered, but his rule ended with the return of the Nubians, who are reputed to have captured him and burned him alive.

Twenty-ninth and Thirtieth Dynasties

(399–343 BC) Two dynasties in the LATE PERIOD. For a period of almost half a century there was a succession of somewhat shadowy kings, none of whom was able to take a grasp of affairs in the way that many predecessors had done when the country's affairs seemed to be distracted. Egypt as a state was embarked on an inexorable decline. Mercenary generals and captains exercised influence, formed competing factions, and sought to make their own fortunes. The Twenty-ninth Dynasty, centred on MENDES, in the DELTA between Busiris and TANIS, comprised Nepherites I, Psammuthis, Achoris and Nepherites II. In international affairs, Egypt played a subsidiary part, with the brunt of opposition to Persia being taken by the Greek states. Indeed, the Persians simply regarded Egypt as a rebelled satrapy, to be brought back into line as soon as possible, and not as an independent state. The first king of the Thirtieth Dynasty, NECTANEBO I, lord of Sebennytos (modern Sammanud), made a valiant effort to restore the form of the Saite kingdom and encouraged Greek mercenaries to leave the country. Nectanebo I was clearly in control of the whole country, since his buildings can be found from PHILAE down to BUBASTIS in the Delta. During his reign there was a serious attempt by the Persians—using Athenian help—to regain Egypt, which was thwarted by dissension between the Persians and their Greek allies, delaying their march on MEMPHIS and enabling Nectanebo to rally his forces. In the ensuing period of peace, Nectanebo's Egypt saw a revival of the arts, on the Saite model but on a lesser scale. The temple precincts at KARNAK were restored and the temple of ISIS at PHILAE begun. Nectanebo's son, Tachos (ruled 362–360 BC), renewed alliance with the Greek states and invaded Syria with an army composed of Egyptians, Athenians and Spartans. To finance this expedition, he levied heavy taxes and suffered consequent unpopularity. He was abandoned in mid-campaign by his grandson, NECTANEBO II, who defected back to Egypt, leaving Tachos to surrender to the Persians. NECTANEBO assumed the throne, putting down a rebellion from MENDES, where the lord still aspired to the kingship, with the help of Sparta. His building record surpassed that of NECTANEBO I, with over 100 sites showing evidence of building work from his reign. He was a particular adherent of bull cults, propagating the Buchis bull cult at ARMANT as well as the APIS cult at Memphis. He held out against increasing Persian pressure until 343 BC, when the Persians returned in overwhelming force and resumed their overlordship. Nectanebo fled south and kept up an appearance of rule in exile, probably in Lower NUBIA, for at least two years, but Egypt was again a satrapy.

Twenty-second and Twenty-third Dynasties

(945–715 BC) Two dynasties in the THIRD INTERMEDIATE PERIOD. The first king was Shoshenq (Bibilical Shishak), a Libyan by descent. He was a leader of the Libyan community that had first come to Egypt partly as slave-prisoners from the armies defeated by Rameses III, partly as mercenaries hired by the Egyptians. His power centre was HERAKLEOPOLIS, in MIDDLE EGYPT, between

THEBES and the DELTA, and he found it easy to extend his power northwards, eventually making his capital at BUBASTIS. Under the Libyans, kingship was a military dictatorship, and the Egyptian peasantry went about their daily work just as they had done under the rule of the HYKSOS. Shoshenq became wealthy by a raid on the kingdom of Judah in which he sacked the Temple at Jerusalem and departed with the riches of Solomon. The descendants of Shoshenq reigned undisturbed until 825 BC, when another branch set up the Twenty-third Dynasty, based at Thebes. These ruled in parallel, but the division was a sign of weakness in the structure, and local governors once again claimed hereditary and independent power.

Twenty-seventh Dynasty

(525–404 BC) A dynasty under the first Persian occupation. Egypt became a satrapy of the vast empire, under the control of a satrap or governor. As it was the richest satrapy by far, the Persian monarchs took a considerable interest in its affairs and government. They assumed the title and style of pharaohs, as legitimate monarchs of Egypt, and did not attempt to alter the institutions and customs of the country. Cambyses (ruled 525–522 BC) was regarded as the founder. Although Egyptian propaganda after the Persian period depicts him as an impious and savage invader, he seems in fact to have behaved with restraint, and there is evidence of his having supported local cults and having built and added to temples. He invaded NUBIA in a catastrophic campaign in which his entire army perished. He was followed by DARIUS I (522–486 BC). The Egyptians were not quiescent under the Persian rule, and Darius came in person in 518 BC to put down an uprising. This seems to have been caused by reaction to a heavy-handed and over-ambitious satrap, Aryandes, whom Darius had executed. Darius introduced a number of reforms. By now coinage was in use in Egypt, introduced by the Persians, although the trading ports had probably been using money for some time before. He built a temple to AMUN-RA in the oasis of el-Kharga. Four years after the Greeks defeated Persia at Marathon, the Egyptians again rebelled, and Darius's successor, Xerxes I (ruled 486–465 BC), arrived to crush it. The continuing struggle between Greeks and Persians encouraged the Egyptians in further efforts at resistance, and there was a large-scale rising against Artaxerxes I (ruled 465–424 BC), with a temporary victory won at Pepremis in the Delta, with the help of the Athenians. The satrap was killed, but the satrap of Syria was despatched with a large army to regain control, and Persian rule continued through the reign of Darius II (424–405 BC) and into that of Artaxerxes II (405–359 BC). In 404 BC, with the Persian empire under threat at its very heart, a Saite lord, Amyrtaeus, succeeded in expelling the Persian satrap and his garrison (*see* TWENTY-EIGHTH DYNASTY). *See also* FIRST PERSIAN OCCUPATION.

Twenty-sixth Dynasty

(672–525 BC) A dynasty in the LATE PERIOD that assumed power under the shadow of Assyrian domination. The first king was Necho I (ruled 672–664 BC), a descendant of the resolute Tefnakht. As a DELTA lord, he had collaborated with Senna-cherib and ASSURBANIPAL and had been rewarded with GOLD and honours. He has been criticized for this, but he had no reason to support the Nubians. The capital was SAIS, and this dynasty is often referred to as the Saite Dynasty. His son, PSAMMETICHUS I, shook off the dominion of the Assyrians and re-established a wholly independent Egypt. He penetrated Assyria as far as their fortress of Ashdod, with an ARMY composed very largely of Greek mercenaries. UPPER EGYPT was under the control of the governor, Mentuemhat, a diplomatist who in his time had seen Nubian and Assyrian overlords come and go. Psammetichus made careful and pacific moves in order to establish his own control in UPPER EGYPT, whose spiritual leader, the chief PRIESTESS of AMUN (*see* ADORATRICE OF AMUN) was a daughter of the great PIANKHY. The national spirit revived rapidly, and the Saite Dynasty presided over a renaissance of artistic and religious life which, in typical Egyptian manner, manifested itself in a determined return to the traditional ways and imitation of the splendours of the past. After the long foreign domination there was a degree of xenophobia, and foreign ways and foreign gods were abandoned in the search for a return to a true Egyptian identity. The cult of PTAH became prominent, as did that of the Saite protective goddess NEITH. The OLD KINGDOM was looked to as a model, and the PYRAMID TEXTS were favoured over the more recent BOOK OF THE DEAD as a reliable passport to the AFTERLIFE. Psammetichus's son, Necho II (ruled 610–595 BC), pursued an ambitious foreign policy. The situation in the Near East had altered dramatically. The Assyrians had been broken by the Medes, and the Egyptian king now became their ally against the Babylonians. Necho II destroyed the army of Judah under Josias, set up Joiakim as a puppet king, then marched into Syria. Briefly it seemed as if the empire was restored. But in 605 BC, Necho's army was routed by Nebuchadnezzar, king of Babylon, at Carchemish, and Palestine was annexed by Babylon. Necho's successor, Psammetichus II (ruled 595–589 BC), directed his attention southwards, sending an expedition as far as the second cataract. His successor, Apries (ruled 589–570 BC), made war on the Phoenician cities of Tyre and Sidon, perhaps more in the pursuit of trading disputes than with any thought of re-establishing a Palestinian empire. Many Jewish refugees entered Egypt at this time (the period of the Babylonian Captivity). Apries was ultimately overthrown by his own general, Amasis (ruled 570–526 BC), who held off a Babylonian attack by Nebuchadnezzar and kept the state in prosperity. For all the vicissitudes of changing rulers and dynasties, the Egyptian state had continued in being for far longer than any other and had already seen empires such as those of the Hittites and Assyrians rise and fall. Now, from beyond Babylon, a new empire was flexing its muscles. Amasis observed the rise of Persia and formed alliances with old enemies, including Babylon, to contain it. But the Persians, under Cyrus, defeated the Babylonians and the Lydians, and then turned their attention to Egypt. A new pharaoh, Psammetichus III (ruled 526–525 BC), had just assumed the throne when, under Cambyses, guided across SINAI by the Bedouin and assisted by the treachery of Greek mercenaries, the Persians utterly defeated the Egyptians at PELUSIUM. When Cambyses took MEMPHIS, Psammetichus killed himself.

Twenty-third Dynasty *see* TWENTY-SECOND AND TWENTY-THIRD DYNASTIES.

Two Ladies name
One of the sequence of five NAMES denoting the title of a particular king. The Two Ladies are the vulture goddess Nekhbet (UPPER EGYPT) and the cobra-goddess WADJET (LOWER EGYPT).

Twosre
The last female king of Egypt (ruled 1196–1188 BC), she took power in the turbulent and anarchic period at the end of the NINETEENTH

Twosre

DYNASTY, after the death of her stepson, Siptah. Twosre had the support of the VIZIER, a shadowy figure named Bay or Iarsu, who has left a sinister reputation as a plunderer of the TREASURY he was supposed to safeguard. Documents relating to the reign are few, but Twosre appears to have sent expeditions to SINAI and Palestine, and to have built or added to temples at Heliopolis and Thebes. Her successor, Sethnakhte, described her as a usurper (not necessarily because of her gender) and appropriated for himself the tomb she had built in the VALLEY OF THE KINGS.

U

underworld

During the OLD KINGDOM, life after death for the vast majority of the population was assumed to be located in the underworld, a vast, gloomy, ill-defined region where spirits wandered, deprived both of the splendour of heaven and the material pleasures of life on earth. Although it contrasted with the fate of a dead king, who ascended to the sky to join the gods, it was not a hell in the later Christian sense, as entry there was inevitable and not governed by any kind of choice or moral practice; nor was it a place of punishment. By the end of the OLD KINGDOM, this concept of the underworld began to lose its force. The slight 'democratization' of society was a factor, as was the growing independence of NOMARCHS, who were building greater tombs for themselves and associating them with local as well as national deities. The development and popularity of the OSIRIS legend played a part, although here cause and effect are difficult to distinguish. The old idea was replaced by the notion of an underworld open to all, although not to be entered without some difficulty. Situated beneath the valley of the NILE and parallel to it, it could only be entered through a narrow gorge in a mountain range. This intermediate area was a dangerous and fearful place, inhabited by demons and monsters. Safe passage for the traveller, in his spirit-boat, was not guaranteed. He passed through a succession of gates where the correct phrases must be uttered, or entry would be refused. In such a situation, the correct phrases on papyrus scrap, tomb wall or coffin lid could drive off the demons and make the passage easy. At last he reached the realm of OSIRIS, but his ordeals were not yet over. He must undergo the Judgement of the Dead, which took place in the Hall of MAAT, goddess of truth and harmony. In the scales of Maat, the deceased's heart was weighed against her divine feather. While the heart was being weighed, and its owner prayed for a good result and for his heart not to traduce him, a varied company looked on. This included THOTH himself, who wrote down the result of the Judgement, whilst ANUBIS, assisted by WEPWAWET, adjusted the scales. A devouring monster, with a CROCODILE head and a body composed of lion and hippopotamus, waited nearby in case the judgement should be adverse. The candidate had to make a form of 'negative' confession, enumerating a list of 42 bad or undesirable actions that he had not committed in his lifetime. This was read out to a court of 42 assessor-gods (the same number as the total of the NOMES). When the Judgement was complete and satisfactory (as the papyri and murals show it to have always been), the dead person was ushered by HORUS into the presence of Osiris, prince of the underworld, and was free to pursue his future existence. The realm of the underworld was assumed to be like that of Egypt, with the reeds and fields, the houses and temples, the waterways, and all the pleasures and pursuits of mortal life, including work. But work in the underworld was a pleasure, not a duty. *See also* AFTERLIFE, DEATH.

Upper Egypt

The long, narrow valley of the NILE from MEMPHIS to the first cataract, forming one of the original two lands that comprised the ancient Egyptian kingdom. Its chief centre was THEBES. Its ancient emblem was the SEDGE or lily.

uraeus

An ornamental serpent worn on the brow, emblematic of the snake-goddess WADJET or BUTO, and symbol of kingship from the early LOWER EGYPT kingdom. *See also* REGALIA.

Userkaf *see* FIFTH DYNASTY.

V

Valley of the Kings

A steep-sided, rocky valley in the arid hills on the west bank of the NILE, opposite THEBES. The EIGHTEENTH-DYNASTY king TUTHMOSIS I inaugurated the practice of royal burial here in an effort to protect the tombs against the depredations of TOMB ROBBERS, and it was used for 400 years. A barrier was built across the entrance to the valley and was put under permanent guard. Rock-cut tombs go back to early times, and there were superb MIDDLE-KINGDOM examples at BENI-HASAN. The tombs in the Valley of the Kings were much more ambitious. That of Tuthmosis I was a three-chambered one, but the later ones are more complex. The general plan comprised a steep descending entrance stair, ending in an anteroom. Beyond this was a large pillared hall with store rooms for the funerary items and accessories. The entrances were concealed at first, but since this did not save the tombs from robbery, reliance was placed later on formidable defences and secret passages. The Ramessid pharaohs sought to outdo all others with their tombs, as with other constructions. That of Sethos I has a great hall nearly 200 metres (650 feet) long.

A consequence of the decision to place royal tombs in this remote valley was that the tomb and the MORTUARY TEMPLE were inevitably far apart from each other. Previously, the temple had been placed immediately adjacent to the PYRAMID or MASTABA.

Now the KA of the dead king had to travel a long way to inspect and receive its offerings in the mortuary chapel.

Valley of the Queens

Funerary site at THEBES, in the hills above MEDINET HABU and close to DEIR EL MEDINA, where queens' tombs were situated.

valley temple *see* FUNERARY PRACTICE.

viceroy

From the EIGHTEENTH DYNASTY the office of viceroy of NUBIA was created, assuring the rule of Egypt as far as the fourth cataract. The viceroy's court was a replica of that of the imperial capital but with authority on civil matters only.

vizier

The highest office under the king. The post goes back to the Second Dynasty in the OLD KINGDOM. The vizier's duties were chiefly concerned with the administration of justice, but he was head of all administration and had a vast staff, with ramifications all over the country. Often the vizier was a member of the royal family, perhaps the son of a junior queen, who had shown special ability.

W

Wadjet

A serpent-goddess, protector of the UPPER EGYPT nome called after her, with the cult centre at BUTO.

waste disposal

Every Egyptian settlement was liberally supplied with RUBBISH MOUNDS, which may have been a nuisance at the time as well as a convenience but which have proved to be treasuries for the archaeologist, even though every object in them, other than the very smallest, is broken. They reveal much about the everyday life of the town, the utensils and equipment used, even the DIET of the people.

water clock

This was invented in the reign of AMENOPHIS I (EIGHTEENTH DYNASTY) by one Amenemmes, virtually the only inventor recorded by name in dynastic history. It is a device for measuring the passage of time by the flow of water from a marked vessel. *See also* TIME.

water supply

The inhabited NILE Valley stretched for several miles on each side of the river, and settlements that could not draw directly on the stream had to make other arrangements. In some cases, in the NEW KINGDOM, wells were sunk, sometimes to considerable depth, and were equipped with a spiral stair to enable water-carriers with their pottery jars to reach the water level, up to 50 metres (164 feet) below ground level. Wells were not found everywhere; many places depended on a supply of water brought in by donkey from a well or water hole beyond the boundary.

Weni

A courtier and high official of the SIXTH DYNASTY. He served under the first three pharaohs of the dynasty but is particularly associated with PEPY I. In his tomb at ABYDOS was found a form of autobiography that sheds much light on the career of a royal official in the OLD KINGDOM. The autobiographical details are incidental to the main purpose of the work, which is to praise Weni and show to the AFTERLIFE that he had an exemplary career. Beginning as an administrator on the royal estates, he was brought into the palace as a groom of the bedchamber of King Pepy I. Promoted to the rank of King's Friend, he was given the task of superintending the construction of Pepy's PYRAMID city. He was then made a judge and worked closely with the VIZIER, proclaiming that he often discussed secret matters with the vizier alone. He was given the high status of Unique Friend and employed on the delicate and secret task of investigating a plot in the harem involving the queen. 'His Majesty made me go in to hear it alone. No chief judge and vizier, no official was there, only I alone, because I was worthy, because I was rooted in His Majesty's heart, because His Majesty filled his heart with me . . . Never before had one like me heard a secret of the king's harem.' Having performed this task satisfactorily, Weni was then made a general and put at the head of a punitive expedition sent eastwards against the Bedouin and Libyans. This was successful, and he led a further raid into southern Palestine. Describing this, Weni records, 'His Majesty sent me at the head of this army, there being counts, royal seal-bearers, sole companions of the palace, chieftains and MAYORS of towns of UPPER and LOWER EGYPT, companions, leaders of scouts, chief priests of Upper and Lower Egypt, from the villages and towns that they governed and from the Nubians of those foreign lands'. Outliving his master, Pepy, he also served Merenra I, who created a governorship for him. His final task was to supervise the gathering of ALABASTER for the decoration of Merenra's PYRAMID at Saqqara. One of the many marks of royal favour that he notes was that Pepy provided him with a splendid SARCOPHAGUS of fine TURA limestone. Weni's narrative reveals the different tasks that a career official might be asked to undertake and demonstrates the resourcefulness and energy of such men. Above all it reveals the utter and complete worshipful loyalty he felt to the kings he served. Although couched in the conventional phraseology of all such 'autobiographical' texts, there is no reason to doubt its sincerity.

Wenis

Last PHARAOH of the FIFTH DYNASTY, his rule ending around 2460 BC. It is generally taken to mark the end of the classic period of the OLD KINGDOM. Wenis's funerary complex at northern Saqqara, restored in the reign of Rameses II, was so grand as to give him the status of a local deity in later times.

Wepwawet

A deity of the UNDERWORLD, a jackal- or wolf-headed god, the 'opener of the ways'. His origin was as the NOME deity of ASYUT, and, with ANUBIS, he was recognized as protector of the NECROPOLIS at ABYDOS.

ing, were pursued largely by women; this seems to have included the economically important business of milling corn. But generally, women were relegated to supporting or subservient roles in public life, as MUSICIANS, dancers and sacred or secular PROSTITUTES. *See also* ADORATRICE OF AMUN, CHILDBIRTH, PRIESTESSES.

writing

The Egyptians evolved their own style of writing over a lengthy period, beginning far back in the Naqada phase of the PRE-DYNASTIC era. Study of decorated pottery remains reveals a progression of illustration from representation towards greater stylization and finally the emergence of pure symbol, as in the emblems denoting particular gods. It was a slow and gradual process, and there was no single moment at which it could be said, 'today writing has been invented'. Rather, writing crept up on society, as the increasingly intricate and stylized ART of design was found to be capable of containing and passing on more complex messages. The initial purpose was the utilitarian one of keeping records and assigning property. Egyptian writing omitted the vowel sounds and rendered consonants only, causing speculation about which vowels were in use in certain words or names, hence the alternative spellings of RA as Re, and many other examples. There were two additional forms of writing to supplement the original HIEROGLYPHICS. HIERATIC was a cursive form of hieroglyphics, used in accounting and administration and for annotating hieroglyphics, in use from the late OLD KINGDOM period. DEMOTIC was a later version of hieratic, from the 7th century BC. In the schools, hieratic was the first form of writing to be taught. The pupil would learn by copying symbols

White Chapel *see* SESOSTRIS I.

White Crown *see* CROWN; REGALIA.

White Granary *see* GRANARY; TRADE.

White House *or* **Treasury** *see* CHANCELLOR; TREASURY.

White Nile

The longer of the two branches of the NILE, rising in Lake Victoria in Central Africa.

White Walls

An early name for the site that was later called MEMPHIS.

women

The dynastic world was male-oriented government, the priesthood, the learned professions, were male preserves. Whatever her natural abilities and her ambitions, very few women could break this established order of things. Occasionally one such, finding herself in a strategic situation, could manoeuvre events to her own will. Queen HATSHEPSUT was one, but there were few others of similar stature. Women's rights were ranked below men's, but they were not negligible, and women were not their husband's chattels. The status of women in ancient Egypt was higher than in any comparable empire or culture of the ancient world. In the eyes of the law, it appears that women and men, at least within the same social grouping, were equal. A woman could make her own will, which demonstrated that she had property that was her own. She could sell this property or buy more (including slaves). She could live on her own, without a male 'guardian'. Certain trades, not only in those areas of activity always entrusted to women, midwifery, COSMETICS, child-car-

X Z

Xerxes I *see* TWENTY-SEVENTH DYNASTY.

Xois
A settlement in the Nile DELTA, between BUSIRIS and BUTO; the home of the FOURTEENTH DYNASTY.

Zoser *or* **Djoser** *see* THIRD DYNASTY.

with a reed pen on to an OSTRACON, or occasionally with a stylus on a clay tablet. Writing on papyrus was reserved for the more important documents.

writing materials

PAPYRUS was the principal writing material but beaten-out leather sheets and wooden boards were also used, as were clay tablets, in which the letters would be scratched with a stylus. Ink was not a liquid but was manufactured in the form of little cakes of paste and pigment, similar to modern watercolour paints, and held on a small rectangular palette. The most common colours are black and red, although writing is also found in yellow, blue, green and white on variously coloured backgrounds. The writing instrument was a fibrous reed brush, its tip filed or shaped according to the degree of fineness required.